THE CEO AND CRO SALES PLAYBOOK FOR EARLY SAAS SUCCESS

WINNING AT SaaS

STEVE TAFARO

Tafaro & Associates, Inc.
stafaro@stevetafaro.com

ISBN: 979-8-9902476-0-4 (paperback)
ISBN: 979-8-9902476-1-1 (ebook)

Ordering Information:
Special discounts are available on quantity purchases by corporations, associations, and others. For details, contact; stafaro@stevetafaro.com

I like to win! *Winning at SaaS* is dedicated to those who are responsible for accelerating sales growth and shareholder value in an early-stage SaaS company. If you like to win, you'll like what I have to say.

CONTENTS

Foreword vii

Introduction xi

Chapter 1: Generating Revenue and Profitability
            in a SaaS Business 1

Chapter 2: Creating Alignment within Your
            Organization 9

Chapter 3: Implementing the Tafaro Growth
            Accelerator Sales Process 13

Chapter 4: Designing a Marketing Foundation for
            Rapid Growth 19

Chapter 5: Building A Sales Foundation 45

Chapter 6: Developing An Account Management
            Foundation 71

Conclusion 83

Resources and Learning 87

Appendix A: Aligning with the Buying Team 89

Appendix B: Executive Buyer Conversations 93

Appendix C: Value-Based Selling 97

Appendix D: Creating a Solution Image........................ 101

Appendix E: The Overview Demo and
                 the Working Demo 105

Appendix F: Frequently Asked Questions...................... 109

Appendix G: An Investor's Guide for Managing Risk.... 113

Acknowledgments 117

Endnotes 119

FOREWORD

In the fast-paced arena of the digital age where software as a service (SaaS) reigns supreme, crafting a sales organization that thrives requires a blueprint that goes beyond the conventional: *The CEO and CRO Sales Playbook for Early SaaS Success* isn't just a book—it's a strategic playbook that illuminates the path to implementing the **Tafaro Growth Accelerator**™, a sales and marketing system that stands as a beacon of success in the SaaS landscape.

In the journey to establish and elevate a SaaS sales organization, there's no room for complacency. The realm of SaaS sales demands innovation, adaptation, and an unwavering commitment to new clients and customer-centricity. With this definitive playbook in your hands, you're equipped with a treasure trove of insights and strategies, but most importantly, practical wisdom from a seasoned software veteran, Steve Tafaro. Tafaro's 45 years of experience span from the early days of IBM and Oracle to the modern-day vertical SaaS companies that have scaled and delivered by focusing on sales excellence.

Highlighting the success of seasoned experts, *Winning at SaaS* draws back the curtain on the intricate art of designing, building, and scaling a SaaS sales powerhouse. As you traverse through these pages, you'll find yourself immersed in a world where every facet of the sales process is meticulously examined and measured, from prospecting to nurturing, from closing to delighting—each step imbued with the essence of customer-centricity.

This book does not merely preach the principles of sales excellence; it demonstrates them through vivid case studies and real-world examples that breathe life into the strategies outlined within. These narratives are not just anecdotes; they are guideposts that illuminate the path toward establishing the kind of customer relationships that propel SaaS organizations beyond the ordinary.

As the founder of a successful vertical SaaS company focused on the financial and professional services markets, I have seven years of direct experience implementing the **Tafaro Growth Accelerator** strategy and playbook. His methods delivered aggressive growth and market leading outcomes in a highly competitive landscape.

Customer-centricity, a cornerstone of this blueprint, isn't just a buzzword—it's a guiding principle that transforms transactions into partnerships. *Winning at SaaS* invites you to challenge traditional sales paradigms, urges you to embrace empathy, pushes you to understand customer pain points, and helps you chart a course that anticipates their needs even before they do.

At the heart of every successful sales organization lies technology, and this book doesn't shy away from embracing the digital tools that empower modern sales teams. The digital age demands a harmonious marriage of human ingenuity and technological prowess, and within these pages, you'll find insights into how to leverage analytics to supercharge your sales efforts.

But this isn't a one-size-fits-all manual—it's a playbook that empowers you to tailor strategies to your unique SaaS offering, target market, and growth stage. As you navigate through the chapters, you'll discover that the real power lies not just in the strategies themselves, but in the art of adaptability—an art that sets exceptional SaaS sales organizations apart from the rest.

We owe a debt of gratitude to Steve Tafaro for his commitment to unraveling the complexities of SaaS sales and crafting this masterful playbook. The collective expertise of Tafaro and his guests, honed through years of hands-on experience, shines through these pages, offering a compass that navigates the tumultuous seas of SaaS sales with unwavering clarity.

As you embark on the voyage through *Winning at SaaS,* you may find that you're not only inspired, but now have gained a strategic arsenal that empowers you to design, build, and scale a sales organization to an exceptional level. May this book serve as your steadfast companion, your guiding light, and your secret weapon as you architect a customer-centric SaaS sales powerhouse.

Enjoy the journey,

Ben Harrison
Cofounder, DealCloud

INTRODUCTION

The SaaS market is on the rise and the number of SaaS companies in existence is naturally following suit. In their market research report published in June 2023, Fortune Business Insights projects the global software as a service (SaaS) market to grow from $273.55 billion in 2023 to $908.21 billion by 2030, at a CAGR of 18.7%.[1]

Although SaaS start-ups have become increasingly popular, Forbes states that 90% of SaaS start-ups will fail to achieve the desired level of success and fail to generate adequate revenue.[2] One of the primary reasons is inadequate marketing and sales efforts.

For early-stage companies, sales growth is the leading indicator of future performance and value accretion. When it comes to sales and marketing, I've seen far too many SaaS companies with great innovative solutions fail—not based on their products, but because of weak marketing and ill-equipped and trained sales and service teams.

If you're an executive responsible for the growth of an early-stage SaaS business, this book can be an extremely valuable resource to you. You'll hear from executives of successful SaaS companies who have built their businesses from inception to market leaders, and from investors who provide valuable insight as to how to maximize shareholder value.

My name is Steve Tafaro. I'm the founder of Tafaro & Associates, Inc., and I've been in the software business for over 45 years. I've spent the past 33 years helping software and technology services organizations build the capabilities necessary to accelerate sales growth and improve business value.

Winning at SaaS is the playbook I've helped SaaS companies follow to sustainable growth and life-changing success. My purpose here is to share with you the sales and marketing foundations, tools, and skills that make up the **Tafaro Growth Accelerator**, the system that was adopted and mastered by these companies to accelerate growth and return value to investors.

Today, success is measured in weeks and months, not years. Flawless execution is needed by all parts of the organization to achieve profitability—to win.

The content within *Winning at SaaS* is based on years of learning from prominent experts and has been rigorously tested, refined, and proven in real-world laboratories of companies just like yours. It's built around the core belief that sales and marketing are two sides of the same coin and must be viewed as a unified process in which strategy and tactics are aligned within the company. This results in a full organizational commitment to winning new business, maintaining the highest degree of customer satisfaction, and continuously adding value.

In the following chapters, you'll learn about the **Tafaro Growth Accelerator,** which includes the foundations, tools, and skills that will make your sales and marketing teams your greatest assets. If you follow the recommendations in this playbook, everyone involved will learn to execute the strategies and techniques necessary to build strong relationships with today's buyers and give them the peace of mind and confidence to choose you.

This playbook will help you build an agile, customer-centric SaaS sales growth engine for your company.

Comments from the Experts

"As identified in this introduction, running a SaaS software company is fundamentally different from running either a business that delivers products one at a time or provides more traditional IT services.

"The successful sales model leans heavily on truly understanding the business value that your solution is providing to the client from *their* point of view while thinking about all sales in terms of the lifetime value of that relationship.

"Having a sales process that leverages the expertise of multiple individuals in a disciplined, execution-oriented framework is key to sustained success. Relying on solo sales 'stars' that go it alone, or the consulting approach that assumes that potential clients will be drawn to your expertise without a comprehensive sales framework to drive revenue attainment, are both doomed to yielding subpar results in the real world of the competitive SaaS marketplace."

–Bob Farina, CEO at Magna5

"I've spent most of my career on the operator side as the CEO of technology businesses and have recently made the move to the venture investor side. Steve and I first connected during my time as the CEO of iLevel.

"iLevel was a disrupting technology in the private equity sector and was the first offering for portfolio management to the PCM (private capital market). This was a complex, multi-constituent technology sale that required a rigid process. After the sale of iLevel, I became CEO of DealCloud, where Steve and I reconnected and implemented his strategy there. This time we did it on a larger scale with a larger addressable market, which included the PCM and investment banks. The process worked well again, and we were able to achieve another successful exit.

"I spend my time now as an early-stage investor in high growth B2B SaaS businesses investing capital and offering operating experience to help these businesses grow and succeed. In almost all instances, construction of the go-to-market strategy is an essential part of the investment thesis.

"Most early-stage SaaS businesses and entrepreneurs need a playbook to guide them to what I refer to as a predictable sales pipeline and methodology. It's essential to put this in place early on to get confidence in how a business will grow and manage all the other aspects of the operation. Predictability is the key, and the **Tafaro Growth Accelerator** is an effective methodology to help guide a management team and their investors. It's a critical factor in managing growth and expectations for management teams."

–Rick Kushel, managing partner at FINTOP Capital

CHAPTER 1

GENERATING REVENUE AND PROFITABILITY IN A SAAS BUSINESS

In the past, software was sold like any other product. It was a capital expense that customers would amortize, usually over a five-year period. Software providers collected most revenue dollars soon after securing a purchase order, with a minor portion of revenue coming from annual maintenance contracts. But other than providing this service, the relationship with the customer was somewhat casual. To grow revenue, software companies had to find new customers in order to boost performance quarter after quarter. This required a high-powered sales organization skilled in closing new accounts.

Today, cloud-based SaaS companies deliver their

solutions in the form of renewable, annual subscriptions. Regardless of the total contract value (TCV) of the license agreement a customer signs, revenues are recognized month by month. For example, let's say a customer signs a three-year license agreement worth $72,000 with a monthly fee of $2,000. In this example the amount *booked* would be a TCV of $72,000.

Bookings is a forward-looking metric that indicates the amount a customer is committed to paying over a given period. *Revenue* can only be recognized when a performance obligation is satisfied. In our example, $2,000 of revenue can be recognized every month. Revenue recognition is the process of converting *bookings* into *revenue*.

Since revenue is recognized month by month, early-stage SaaS companies require more upfront capital than traditional software product companies. They are forced to underwrite the delay in payment while they build and operate the network required to provide their services. By nature, SaaS companies have a longer path to profitability, as their upfront costs are higher while their upfront payments are lower.

On the positive side, because they are already contracted the *bookings* number provides investors with a clear visibility into future revenues. Therefore, *bookings* are often considered to be the most important metric of sales growth and value accretion for early-stage SaaS companies. Once profitable, they become a preferred investment vehicle for the following reasons:

1. Revenue is predictable as the *bookings* number increases.

2. Growth is organic and comes from service usage,

cross-selling, and upselling within their existing accounts.

3. They are inherently scalable, since the cost of serving each customer goes down as growth increases.

To achieve this level of excellence, it is of course very important for an early-stage SaaS company to have a competitive software solution. More important, however, are the strategy and tactics deployed among your sales, account management, and marketing teams. To succeed, they must be tightly aligned with a full organizational commitment to winning new business, maintaining the highest degree of customer satisfaction, and continuously selling and adding value.

This is especially important in today's hypercompetitive and constantly changing sales environment. The evolution in communication and information access has dramatically altered how buying decisions are made, making it more difficult for early-stage companies to win new business and grow existing revenue.

For instance, websites are packed with information about your competitors' products, services, and testimonials, and are constantly being optimized to reach their target audience. Through social networks, prospective buyers can tap into personal connections for references and product reviews. If you read Hubspot's 2023 Sales Trend Report, it clearly points out how companies are finding new ways to blend technology into their marketing and sales processes.[3] As artificial intelligence (AI) evolves, it will help answer questions that will guide buyers and empower their decision-making.

Worldwide Business Research, a firm dedicated to

educating, supporting, and connecting the leadership of the world's core industries, states that "B2B buyers are 57 to 70 percent through their buying research before contacting sales."[4] In their official blog, HubSpot states that "57 percent of today's buyers are less dependent on salespeople during the decision-making process."[5] Another HubSpot blog entry states, "60 percent of buyers want to connect with sales during the consideration phase—after they've created a shortlist of vendors."[6]

The good news is that buyers rarely make decisions solely on information provided over the internet. Ultimately, buyers will interact with a salesperson or account manager to make an informed and confident decision. When they do, they expect to receive immediate value. This is where traditional sales methods fall short.

Focusing internally on your products and services will not always result in buyer interest. Prospective buyers are expecting the people they engage with to understand their business issues and concerns and to offer viable options that not only address these problems but also create value in the process.

Customers need to be comforted and know that your company is capable of and committed to addressing their future needs. Therefore, it's vital that your company be viewed as a thought leader in the marketplace, and the content your marketing team produces must be relevant to your customers' prolonged needs. Success is about culture, execution, and the ability to sell value. Everyone in your company must view the relationship with your customers as a perpetual one. Continue to add value and you should have a customer for life.

This book will help you get there!

Comments from the Experts

"SaaS companies are a preferred investment vehicle because there is excellent forward visibility into future revenue and the incremental cost of serving each customer goes down as the user base increases."

–Paul Scura, managing partner at Scura Partners

"The SaaS model is a CFO's best friend because it provides a predictable revenue stream if done correctly. I've had the privilege of working with Steve Tafaro at multiple early-stage SaaS companies and he helped us implement the methodologies outlined in this book. By following the steps in **Tafaro's Growth Accelerator**, we were able to build a predictable, repeatable, and scalable sales engine.

"To maximize valuation, SaaS companies must be able to drive high recurring revenue growth in a capital efficient manner. The early years of a SaaS company are capital intensive. For illustrative purposes, in year one you may spend $1,200,000 on sales and marketing to close $1,000,000 in annual recurring revenue bookings. In addition, you may spend 20% of that annual recurring revenue on support and hosting related expenses.

"Based on that example, you will spend $1,200,000 on sales and marketing and $200,000 in support and hosting costs while only earning $1,000,000 in revenue resulting in a cash burn of $400,000 in the first year. This does not sound like a very good business model.

"Let's now look at year two. The company receives

another $1,000,000 but must only pay support and hosting fees, which again are $200,000. This results in a positive cash flow of $800,000. Year three will be the same as year two with another year of positive cash flows of $800,000. After three years you have a positive cash flow of $1,200,000. This now sounds like a pretty good business model. But it must be done correctly.

"This model becomes even more profitable if you reduce churn, continue to retain the client, and increase that client's annual recurring revenue by following the steps in chapter 6, Developing an Account Management Foundation.

"As a CFO of early-stage companies, you are always dealing with the struggles of limited resources and debating as to where to spend. Because we built a repeatable and scalable sales process by following Tafaro's method, we had the confidence to be able to hit our sales targets. As a result, we were able to build a predictable financial model, which helped in determining when we needed to raise cash, how much cash we needed to raise, and where to spend our cash.

"The ultimate outcome of any SaaS business is to increase the valuation of your company. Obviously, increasing annual recurring revenue is going to increase the value of the company, but it is also important to show that you can grow in an efficient manner that will lead to profitability. Optimizing key metrics such as lower customer acquisition costs, low churn, and high lifetime customer value will result in a much higher multiple on your company's annual recurring revenue and a much higher valuation of the company."

–Jim Weber, president and CFO at DecuSoft, Inc.

Key Takeaways

- Cloud-based SaaS companies deliver their solutions in the form of renewable, annual subscriptions.

- The bookings number provides investors with a clear visibility into future revenues since they are already contracted.

- SaaS businesses are considered a great investment vehicle because they are inherently scalable, revenue is predictable, and growth is organic.

- The strategy and tactics deployed among your sales, account management, and marketing teams must be tightly aligned.

- Prospective buyers are expecting the people they engage with to understand their business issues and concerns and to offer viable options that not only address those issues and concerns but also create value in the process.

CHAPTER 2

CREATING ALIGNMENT WITHIN YOUR ORGANIZATION

Through my years of experience as a consultant and advisor, I learned how important it is to seek alignment with the executives who will be evaluating my performance—whether it's an executive management team or an outside board of directors. Though every individual will have their own opinion of what success will look like, to succeed you must create a united view. As an executive in an early-stage SaaS company, it's critical that you have tight alignment with your management team and create a shared vision as you plan and roll out your go-to-market approach.

Alignment is about culture, leadership, and execution. The first step is to establish the importance of the unified process inherent in *Winning at SaaS* and explain why it's necessary for your success as a SaaS company. As you develop your operational and go-to-market plan, it's critical that your management team have full participation. Your goal here is to begin to instill a culture of performance by giving them equity in the process and the ability to share in the results.

In coaching early-stage SaaS companies, I recommend the following go-to-market imperatives to accelerate growth and build long-term shareholders:

1. **Build a high-powered new accounts sales team.** Although sales professionals and account managers are both required to be proficient in selling, their overall skill set is different. New account salespeople should be confident, goal-oriented, resilient, and tenacious enough to make calls and follow-up. They must ask insightful questions, demonstrate curiosity, actively listen, build trust, and articulate the value of their solutions while building a relationship with the customer.

2. **Develop an account management team to service and be viewed as an asset to your client base.** Account managers draw upon a broad skill set that includes strategic thinking. They need to consider the entire account landscape, understand the various stakeholders, have domain knowledge, identify potential areas where additional services could provide added value, and facilitate the resolution of technical issues. Essentially, they must be a trusted resource with the ability to build close symbiotic relationships with their customers. This will enable them to reduce churn, renew existing licenses, and grow incremental revenue through upselling and cross-selling.

3. **Invest in your digital and content marketing capabilities to establish yourself as the market leader.** SaaS marketing is multi-faceted. Its messaging must be compelling to attract potential users, generate leads, and nurture prospective buyers—all while producing content that is relevant to the prolonged needs of your clients and increasing the lifetime value of a customer. Marketing alone cannot accomplish this and requires tight integration with sales and account management. That's why *Winning at SaaS* presents sales and marketing as "two sides of the same coin."

As you read further, you'll see how the integration of sales and marketing comes to life.

Comments from the Experts

"I love that Steve puts this chapter right up front, because frankly implementing any system (technology or process) takes leadership, and a shared vision is leadership 101, step one. Creating alignment and a shared vision becomes the 'why' we are doing what we are doing, and the constant calibration to that common goal is critical as you encounter both success and challenges. Enlisting all stakeholders in the 'how' to achieve becomes the shared plan with the appropriate systems to support the execution. The **Tafaro Growth Accelerator** presented in *Winning at SaaS* establishes a culture of performance and accountability. Culture begets execution and success. That's why it's important to establish and reinforce this culture as quickly as possible, even at the start-up stage."

–Shannon Dolan, COO at Currence, Inc.

Key Takeaways

- It's critical that you have tight alignment with your management team around a shared vision as you plan and roll out your go-to-market approach.

- Establish the importance of a unified process that includes the following go-to-market imperatives:

  - A high-powered new accounts sales team.

  - An account management team to service and be viewed as an asset to your client base.

  - The digital and content marketing capabilities that will allow you to be recognized as the market leader.

CHAPTER 3

IMPLEMENTING THE TAFARO GROWTH ACCELERATOR SALES PROCESS

The **Tafaro Growth Accelerator** is a sales process configured for new account salespeople and account managers. The process consists of five phases: *Qualify, Verify, Position, Solve,* and *Confirm.* Each phase includes measurable and repeatable selling steps that salespeople and account managers are required to perform before moving a prospect to the next phase.

By executing the process, salespeople and account managers will improve the accuracy, speed, and efficiency of the actions they can control. As they gain experience with the process, every interaction with a buyer will have greater impact and contribute to the objective of building long-term, profitable customer relations.

Implementation consists of the following three-step plan that has been tested and proven to be successful.

Step 1: Education

Every employee in lead development, sales, and account management must learn the foundational elements and principles inherent in the **Tafaro Growth Accelerator.** Knowing how to execute the techniques and processes is also vital for success. As you read through this playbook, you'll see that every aspect of selling to a new or existing client is meticulously laid out, providing you with the educational content that needs to be presented and learned.

Step 2: Personalization and Configuration

Once the *foundational elements* and *principles* are understood, the process can be personalized and configured to fit the needs and objectives of your business, your market, and your customers' buying behavior. Everyone who will be involved in its execution should be invited to provide input to the configuration and personalization effort. As issues are raised, discussed, and resolved, common ground is reached, and ownership of the system belongs to the team members. This is where you build team alignment and equity.

Step 3: Changing Behavior

It's important to remember that you will be requiring salespeople and account managers to shift their methodology from promoting products and services to solving problems, and this requires behavioral change. That's why it's hard. Having worked with hundreds of salespeople and account managers, it's been my experience that when someone learns a new behavior, that behavior needs to be positively reinforced and developed for the person to become proficient at what they've learned. We've all witnessed the tendency for salespeople and account managers to fall back to their old methods after they've been trained in new ones. It happens all the time because the new methods were not practiced and reinforced.

After personalizing and configuring the **Tafaro Growth Accelerator,** it's essential for leadership to measure how each salesperson and account manager is executing the selling steps in each phase. This includes identifying areas requiring remediation and providing ongoing coaching until each salesperson and account manager is executing properly and achieving the expected results.

In my experience, this is best done through one-to-one pipeline reviews conducted twice a month for a period of three months. Once leadership is comfortable with everyone's ability to execute the system properly, monthly reviews and situational sessions will provide the continued reinforcement necessary.

Comments from the Experts

"After reading the *Winning at SaaS* playbook, I find that Steve thoroughly and clearly explains the **Tafaro Growth Accelerator** system, which includes the tactical steps that salespeople and account managers must undertake to win more business and shorten the sales cycle.

"Although every employee in lead development, sales, and account management must learn the *foundational elements* and *principles* inherent in the **Tafaro Growth Accelerator,** and how to execute them, the education process is not as simple as just teaching them the system. It's important to recognize that these employees will be coming to the training sessions with pre-conceived opinions and feelings, and these may not always align with those of management.

"Therefore, I recommend that management spend time discussing the reasons behind the effort, such as why you are implementing the **Tafaro Growth Accelerator,** and the benefits to both the employee and company if the system is successfully implemented. I would also give everyone the opportunity to express their feelings followed by constructive dialogue, which reinforces the decision to implement the system. This will provide a clean slate with which to move forward in a productive manner.

"Also realize that people learn differently. Some are very good listeners and can comprehend and retain much of what they've heard, others need visuals to digest information, while some learn by reading and taking notes. So, it's important to incorporate all learning methods when presenting the system. It's also helpful to get all questions on the table with positive discussion so that the employees feel they have a voice in what is being presented.

"I love the fact that there will be ongoing coaching. The ability to execute what has been taught will take time and patience and requires repetition. There is no doubt that some people will revert to their old styles of selling because that's what they are comfortable doing. Coaches should provide constructive feedback supported by specific examples to improve retention and execution."

–Jill Diener, Vocational Counselor

Key Takeaways

- It is vital for every employee in lead development, sales, and account management to learn the *foundational elements* and *principles* inherent in the **Tafaro Growth Accelerator** sales process.

- If you personalize and configure your sales process, everyone involved in its execution should be invited to provide input so that they have equity in the final process.

- It's critically important that you develop and implement a plan to measure how each salesperson and account manager is executing the process and provide remediation and positive reinforcement where needed.

DESIGNING A MARKETING FOUNDATION FOR RAPID GROWTH

The evolution of communication and information access has dramatically reduced the cost of creating, sending, and storing information—all while vastly increasing its availability. Websites are packed with information about a company's products and services. Through LinkedIn and other social networks, prospects can tap into personal connections for references. Every day buyers are using technology to empower their decision-making and become more educated about the companies from whom they purchase products. The role of marketing continues to grow as well, as new technologies such as artificial intelligence emerge and buying behaviors evolve.

With that said, in my experience the marketing resources and capabilities of early-stage companies are often limited.

To combat this, I've identified six *foundational marketing elements* required for rapid growth. The goal of this concept is to focus on these *elements* and execute them flawlessly. Just remember, sometimes subtraction is better than addition.

1. Assure alignment with sales and account management.

Alignment between sales and marketing means sharing strategy and goals that enable both groups to work together in a unified way. In many companies, marketing focuses on generating leads while sales focuses on closing deals. Once a lead is passed to sales, marketing may never hear about it again. This is a flawed approach.

From a SaaS perspective, you should expect that customers to engage with your company before the initial sale and long after. Remember that *your relationship with a client is perpetual.* For you to be able to deliver value after the initial sale, your clients must know your company will be able to address their long-term needs.

Due to their proximity to the market, salespeople can offer valuable insights into buyer needs and establish how your solutions can address them. Many of my clients regularly host sales and marketing meetings to discuss go-to-market strategies, typical client issues, and the content that would be most relevant.

Centralizing communications via a dedicated tool like Slack or other similar workgroup communication tool will allow everyone to see how marketing is planning to engage prospective buyers. Think of it as having an editorial calendar for each type of outreach in order to show the internal team the frequency of the outreach, the target audience, and the message or content that will create demand.

2. Create demand with digital content aimed at offering solutions to buyer issues.

Generally, B2B marketing focuses on selling solutions to prospects who know what they need and who are ready to buy. In their book, *Selling to the C-Suite*, authors Steve Bistritz and Nick Read state, "Marketing is trying to be seen where customers are looking, but it isn't doing much to create demand where it didn't exist before."[7] They go on to state that "The problem is that most prospects aren't actively searching. They have latent or chronic problems they've learned to live with and must be awakened to the fact that they need to change before they can be pointed in the right direction."

So, how do you awaken latent needs?

Some of the following principles concerning buyer behavior are taken from the book *Conceptual Selling*,[8] written by Robert Miller and Stephen Heiman. In my opinion, this is one of the most helpful books you'll find on the subject of selling. Although the information here accurately reflects the foundation of their thoughts, a much deeper understanding can be attained by reading their complete works.

Principle One: *It's not about your product or service, it's about how your product or service can help prospects address the issues they're dealing with (whether identified or latent). It's about the results or capabilities derived from your solution ... what can be achieved by using your software?* [9]

Use your marketing messaging to arouse curiosity by showing prospects how others have benefited from your solution and how it can resolve the problems and issues they're dealing with. The objective is to make the prospect say to themselves, "That's me."

Demand can be created from both inbound and outbound marketing. My high-growth clients believed that consistent inbound marketing was necessary to attract new accounts and reinforce their presence with current clients. This required frequent blogging that presented their company as an expert in the field and highlighted what prospective buyers could achieve and have achieved by using their software. This was done with social media posts, email campaigns, and mobile-friendly ads.

Today, those clients are also using short-form video to create awareness and generate interest. Video testimonials showcasing satisfied clients validate the value they provide is one way to do this, and have been embedded on their website, put on social media channels, and included in email campaigns.

If you're selling to an identifiable market, using a consistent outbound marketing program that tailors your message to the specific individuals (buyer types) in the companies you target is highly effective.

When a prospect views your website from an inbound campaign and asks for information, you should consider this to be a high priority. When this happens, it's likely that something about your message or blog "touched them," and demand has been created. This could also be the result of a prospect clicking on a link in an outbound email because your message aroused their curiosity. In either case, the prospect wanted to find out more.

Principle Two: *Buyers within an organization will be viewing your solution from their business view. Different buyers have different needs and concerns.*

Mid-level managers will focus on how your solution can help them meet the objectives imposed on them by senior management. Will it reduce costs? Can it be implemented on time and on budget? Is the risk minimal? Will it make them personally successful? When you sell to the mid-level managers you will face more competition, be treated as a commodity, and constantly deal with pricing issues.

C-level executives focus more on strategic organizational issues such as revenue growth, market share, profitability, and competitive positioning. *We advise our clients, whenever possible, to focus their marketing efforts on the needs and issues of executive buyers.* If you can relate your solution to their mindset, you will have less competition, be considered more of a strategic partner, and face fewer price issues. To effectively sell to C-level executives, it's important to understand the key issues they face and know what they look for to gain trust with an organization.[10]

3. Communicate on both a rational and emotional level.

An important concept that often gets overlooked is how the brain functions relative to behavior and decision-making.

Principle Three: *Buying is an emotional decision that prospects make after going through a rational product or service evaluation process. It is key that we influence that emotional decision.*[11]

To illustrate this, I refer to Simon Sinek's book, *Start with Why,*[12] or his TED Talk (same title),[13] which is available on YouTube. Sinek is an author and expert on leadership and the science of decision-making, and I believe the "start with why" concept must be a part of your message architecture.

In his book, Sinek points to the Golden Circle as a perspective about why some organizations have achieved a disproportionate degree of influence versus others.[14] The Circle has three layers. The outer layer describes WHAT their company does. Everyone is easily able to describe the products or services their company sells. The middle layer describes HOW a company does WHAT it does. HOWs are often given to explain how a company's products or services are different or better—their differentiated message or value proposition. The center "core" layer describes WHY a company does WHAT it does. WHY do they exist? What is their purpose, cause, or belief?

When most organizations describe their business, they do so from the outside in, from WHAT to HOW, because it's the clearest way to communicate. Few companies communicate from the inside out because few companies can articulate WHY they do WHAT they do.

Sinek relates the Golden Circle to the major levels of the brain. The neocortex of the brain is responsible for rational and analytical thought and language and corresponds to WHAT a company does. The two middle layers comprise the limbic system, which is responsible for our feelings, such as trust and loyalty, and all decision-making. When we communicate from the outside in, people can understand vast amounts of information, though it does not drive behavior. But when we communicate from the inside out, we're talking directly to the part of the brain that controls decision-making.

Companies that fail to communicate a sense of WHY force buyers to make decisions with only empirical evidence. If a company doesn't have a clear sense of WHY, then it's impossible for prospects and customers to perceive anything more than WHAT the company does. When this happens, manipulations that rely on commodity factors (like price, features, and service) become the primary currency of differentiation. Those decisions take more time and cause buyers to feel uncertain.

Communication that starts with WHY and is reinforced with HOW (the emotional components) allows buyers to go through a rational process. However, it is the HOW and the WHY that bring in the emotional aspects: "I like working with them," "It just feels right," "They seem passionate about what they do." When you're one of two competitors, emotions play a significant role in the decision-making process.

Being able to articulate your WHY and HOW enables you to compete in all levels of decision-making (rational and emotional). Here's an example of the top-level messaging of one of my clients when the company was originally formed:

Our WHY

When it comes to CRM for financial professionals, *company name,* is changing the status quo.

HOW We Do It

Everything we do starts with investors and advisors. From product design through current service delivery and our future product roadmap, the voice of investors and advisors is present.

WHAT We Do

We power your dealmaking process with a platform designed specifically for Private Equity and Investment Banking professionals to seamlessly execute their fundraising, sourcing, and deal management strategies. By going well beyond the limits of generic CRM, our solution stands alone as the most functional, best reporting, and exceptional relationship management solution for deal professionals.

4. Create a Power Index to uncover buyer needs and issues.

Interest can come from many different levels in an organization. It can also be passed down from executives to managers who have been asked to evaluate a product or service. In most cases, interest is often vague. Prospects will say "we know what we want" but may not see the periphery of what they can have, what is available, or other evaluation criteria.

Principle Four: *A sale can only occur if buyers are either looking for a solution to a stated need or willing to discuss the fact that a problem exists. Buyers must agree that there's a discrepancy or* *gap between their "current state" and "where they want to be." If we don't understand the buyers' needs and they have difficulty expressing them, how do we offer solutions that address them?*[15]

To solve this dilemma, I highly recommend that you create a Power Index. A Power Index should list all the capabilities or results a buyer can achieve by using your software and can be sorted by application or functional area. After each capability or result, the buyers are asked to assess whether they are "underpowered" or "adequately powered" in that specific application or functional area.

Here are two examples. One of my clients licenses CRM software to private equity and investment banking firms focused on deal sourcing and fund management. Their software addresses the needs of this vertical market. Hence, their Power Index lists the capabilities for applications like deal origination, sourcing, deal management and execution, fundraising, portfolio and reporting, knowledge management, etc. Below is their Power Index for deal origination and execution for investment bankers.

Deal Origination and Execution	Fully Powered	Under Powered
Track senior professionals' sourcing and origination efforts		
Manage sponsor coverage relationships and related marketing touches		
Manage firm pipeline report		
Manage deal execution and track progress of buyer through the deal marketing process		

Formalize industry groups and end-market coverage		
Institutionalize firm's industry knowledge to equip junior bankers with firm's experience and history		
Dashboards for sponsor and industry coverage delivering relevant relationship information to team members		
Multi-relationship mapping of company, product offering, and end market served to efficiently manage research and pitch efforts		
Establish nomenclature and related tags enabling team to manage information by vertical and practice area		

Below is another client who licenses software for complex compensation processes. This is a horizontal application, so it's sorted by functional areas such as integration, administration, configuration, data and calculations, security and audit, and reporting.

Shown here is the Power Index for Administration and Process:

Administration and Process	Fully Powered	Under Powered
Global compensation view, multiple language, and currencies		
Track compensation awards during the cycle before managers submit for approval		
Allow HR to support their organization leaders in real time through the comp planning process through proxy		

Allow for entry (in multi-currency) of total budget/pool amounts		
Allow for budget restrictions to be imposed on managers, not to exceed the total budget/pool amount allocated to the manager's group		
Track spend against budget in real time, top down or bottoms up		
Allow users to customize their views within their security rights or allow admins to set up a user's view preferences ahead of the cycle open		
Immediately react to changes that affect compensation such as organizational structure, compensation plans, performance measures, data sources and more.		

The Power Index is a highly effective tool because it leads buyers through a rational process, providing them with a clear understanding of the explicit results they can achieve while helping to prioritize results. As buyers go through the process of completing the Power Index, several interesting things happen:

- They'll see the full array of capabilities and results they can achieve—not just the ones they assumed. This expands the inherent value of the software.

- The possibilities as to what the software can deliver and the issues it can resolve will become more apparent.

- If a manager is asked to evaluate competitive solutions and has not developed explicit criteria, the

Power Index often becomes the basis for evaluation, as it is a useful tool to measure others.

By using the Power Index, salespeople and account managers are able to work with each buyer to identify the "gaps" in their current process. It can also be used to show how the software "closes the gaps." Once the buyer understands what the software can deliver, the salesperson and/or account manager can work with the buyer to establish the specific value associated with closing each "gap."

Instead of demonstrating the software and presenting the product features and benefits (the old way of selling), this approach allows the buyer to identify their specific areas of need, which is a far more powerful approach.[16]

5. Implement a pre-sales capability with lead scoring.

The one area where most companies drop the ball is lead follow-up. It's critical that every prospect who shows interest in your inbound or outbound marketing (via their digital behavior) is contacted. Assuming the sales team will follow up with prospective buyers who come to the website, click on a link, or complete an inquiry is a flawed process—and they almost never get contacted.

Over the years I've tested a pre-sales capability that solves this problem while reducing overall sales costs. The pre-sales team is staffed by entry-level employees who desire to be sales professionals in the future. Entry-level people are great to work with because there are no preestablished behaviors that must be overcome and they're eager to learn.

The pre-sales team becomes the link between marketing

and the sales team. Though they report to marketing, there should be constant communication between the groups. Since marketing speaks indirectly to many prospective customers through digital campaigns, it's important to have a method to analyze the digital behavior of your targeted prospects and to score their behavior accordingly. This process enables the pre-sales team to prioritize their follow-up activities.

The pre-sales team must be trained to contact all leads (as per a lead scoring system) with a combination of phone and email follow-up. Everything needs to be scripted—from their talk tracks with prospects to the voice mails they leave and the emails they send. It's also important that you coach your teams to anticipate and respond to every objection and any question a prospective buyer may ask. To accomplish this, you can role-play the entire process until everyone is comfortable. Their job is to contact a prospective buyer and facilitate a call with a sales executive to fill the top of the pipeline. I recommend that you also develop a "playbook" for the pre-sales team that includes the following topics:

- Pre-sales roles and responsibilities

- Top level messaging

- Conducting pre-call research

- VM and email best practices

- Sample emails

- Talk tracks with objection handling.

- Presenting the Power Index

- Answers to FAQs from prospects

- Conducting an *overview demo*

- Selling value

In time, you will see how vital this type of preparation and coaching really is. Essentially, you're placing an inexperienced person on the phone with a prospect for an initial call. Without proper preparation, this scenario would be destined to fail. But because pre-sales team members are eager to achieve and typically do not have preexisting behaviors, if you take the time to prepare them for success they will usually rise to the occasion.

6. Develop a program to nurture prospects who expressed interest but are not ready to engage.

If a prospect has shown interest but is not ready to engage, the pre-sales team should be coached to place them on a nurture list.

There are many reasons that prohibit prospects from moving forward in the sales cycle. They may have to wait until a competitive license agreement expires or for the next budget cycle, for instance. If you continue to reach out and make them aware of your many successes, a relationship will develop through your communications.

I recommend creating separate campaigns for prospects that your pre-sales team is nurturing. This will keep them engaged and aware of your activities in the market. By staying in touch, these nurtured prospects will undoubtedly consider your company when they're ready to engage.

Remember what I said before: success is about culture, execution, and the ability to sell value. Everyone in your company must view the relationship with your customers as a perpetual one, and by continuing to add value you should have a customer for life.

Comments from the Experts

"This chapter checks all the important boxes for successful marketing at its best. It's not about theory anymore. Time and experience confirm engaging, connected, and actionable sales, and marketing programs deliver results.

"The world is filled with people who sell products or services without an understanding of what the buyer needs and why they need it. Buyers become confused or skeptical when you make it about you. They resort to their own research to find 'best fit' sellers.

"Numbers don't lie. Misaligned sales, marketing, and account management goals produce results that impact on the bottom line.

"There is a more effective approach. This book outlines the blueprint to align sales and marketing with the client's true business needs. By understanding business priorities and identifying specific, actionable gaps in business needs, salespeople are then able to engage with the prospect by selling value.

"Time and experience confirm that long-term success comes when the focus goes beyond the product or service, to sell value, establish team credibility, demonstrate business value, and nurture a business relationship.

"Marketing must be strategic and personal. It needs to convey the company's messaging and represent its culture and capabilities authentically, transparently, and comprehensively to generate qualified leads. Marketing must work hand in hand with sales who take leads to the next level through a meaningful, consultative, and successful sales process, fostering long-term buyer relationships.

"When you consider the game-changing partnership forged between content marketing and thought leadership, you have a formula to assure alignment with sales and marketing. Thought leadership is a strategic element in any effective digital marketing strategy. It sets the stage for a business conversation with companies with whom *you* want to do business.

"Thought leadership content which focuses on timely, relevant business topics and is supported by industry research helps companies sort through the noise to zero in on issues and possible solutions that may be impacting their business. Each blog, research paper, article, video, or piece of content tells a relatable story. When recognized for producing legitimate, insightful content with your finger on the pulse of your industry, credibility follows. Relevant and important thought leadership helps drive sales. It can position you as a thought leader in your industry. You can become a 'go to' source for industry press and influencers while educating your target market.

"Incorporating thought leadership into your overall content and marketing strategy allows you to establish credibility and authority with the best fit communities. Through it, you create a larger pool of mentions, references to your organization, shares, and backlinks. Thought leadership and selling value are vital tools for any business to increase brand awareness, strengthen credibility, and attract ideal prospect opportunities for success."

–Laura Hills, president at Encore
Business Strategies, LLC

"A foundational marketing consideration, one that brings Sinek's 'Why, How, and What' Golden Circle 'full circle,' is determining 'for whom.' It's important for any company bringing a SaaS brand into existence to avoid falling into what is considered the 'old marketing mentality'—build a great solution and sell like hell until the audience succumbs and buys.

"That doesn't work today and hasn't worked since the commercial mainstream use of the internet as a learning tool. I'll reference a previous point: '57 to 70 percent of buying decisions are made *before* a prospect engages with a sales-person.'[17] As a result, the once all-knowing, all-seeing sales representative no longer holds the knowledge power that they once did—at least not in the eyes of the prospect. As we embrace the AI age, this point will further exacerbate as we can learn as fast as we can think to ask for information; maybe even faster.

"The new marketing mindset, and one that should be adopted by every SaaS company, is this: Find a target audience and build a solution to specifically meet their unmet or underserved needs.

"Today, the balance of power very much resides in the hands of the prospective buyer in the pre-selling phase. They have access to an abundance of information—too much really. They control the pace, tempo, and timing of when the sales process can occur. They have the power to shut us out, turn us off, or close the door before it can even be opened.

"This is also the basis for why so much marketing fails: It's too seller-centric. It's 'about us' or 'our greatness' or 'the value of our solution,' etc. To be truly effective, it must reside in the buyer's mindset:

What's in it for me?

How will this help me personally?

How will this help my customer?

How can we make more money?

How can we save more money?

How can your solution give me a competitive advantage?

How can your SaaS take away my pain?

"This is why we build target persona profiles in the first place—so that our entire team can clearly understand and visualize who our solution is truly built for.

"For start-up SaaS companies, I would define that persona as an 'early adopter.' Essentially, we're answering the question, 'Who are our very first customers?'

"Once we understand our 'Who,' Sinek's 'Why, How, and What' truly brings a more compelling growth mindset to the entire organization. Beyond the typical persona building (title, location, age, background, and buying sophistication) valuable considerations are—on both a personal and organizational level—the customer's top three responsibilities, concerns (or pains), and goals.

"From there, the SaaS company can map out a messaging framework to speak to how their solution can help them meet their functional responsibilities, alleviate their concerns (or pains), and ultimately help them meet their goals, again both on a personal and corporate level. This becomes the basis of the SaaS marketing messaging platform, from which all content must be based, supported, and continuously reinforced.

"Understanding the 'Who' essentially takes you to the end of the beginning from a marketing perspective. A start but not a finish by any means. Next comes the journey—what we call the 'Brand in the Hand.'

"Think of bringing your SaaS solution to the first generation of excellent customers as a hand, with each finger representing a step toward your SaaS brand's adoption and use.

"In simple terms, 'The Brand in the Hand' is:

1. **Awareness**: 'I see you.' The existence of the brand is known.

2. **Understanding**: 'I understand what you do.' The scope of what the brand can do is recognized.

3. **Distinction**: 'I get how you're different.' The brand's unique benefits, advantages, and differences are clear.

4. **Relevance**: 'I see what you can do for me/us.' The brand's value and importance are realized.

5. **Preference**: 'You're the best solution to my/our need.' When considering all decision-influencing criteria, the brand is viewed as the best choice.

"Only when a prospect goes through the five steps can they truly place their trust in your SaaS solution and, literally and figuratively, place your brand in their proverbial hand. There are three primary methods to growing a B2B organization:

1. Attain more customers.

2. Retain and expand existing customers.

3. Increase buyer frequency.

"The SaaS company inherently has growth method three (buyer frequency) in its delivery model. That's the beauty of the SaaS business. Once up and running, it's far more predictable compared to other business models.

"As a result, the marketing and growth focus is immediately streamlined. We must add new users, keep the ones we have, and when possible, look to expand our share of business with them. With a strong account management and service team, the 'keep' and 'expand' components of the growth focus are well attended to. So, really, marketing's almost singular focus, especially with early-stage SaaS companies, is to create visibility and engagement. That means getting as many prospective users fitting the target persona criteria to see the solution, become intrigued by the possibility of transformative value, and give it a try (the proverbial 'demo').

"As start-up SaaS companies do not have infinite marketing dollars, prioritizing three to five marketing objectives around the early adopter audience and aligning all marketing activities around those objectives will be helpful in making traction while mitigating any wasted marketing investments. If you know your target audience and are directing all marketing to that target with three to five objectives firmly in mind, your chances of marketing misfires are immediately minimized."

–Ed Delia, president & B2B brand
strategist at Delia Associates

"Principles one through four are about product market fit, at the micro level, specific to the client situation. In the next chapter Steve will share where in the sales process you should implement the Power Index to validate product-client need. Sometimes the client is not yet aware they have this problem or challenge or need. It is important to figure out if you are going to spend a lot of time educating the client and raising awareness that they have the problem your solution addresses.

"The Power Index is a critical filtering tool, so you don't waste time on this prospect. Put this prospect [back] into a nurture campaign to do the educating in an automated way. Then you can focus on finding those that are ready to solve for this need.

"The Power Index also helps you get to 'no' sooner. While hearing 'no' from a prospect can be discouraging, remember that a 'no' is really 'not now.' Change your mindset from wanting to convert a 'no' to a 'yes' on the spot. Be grateful when you hear a 'no,' have confidence in your product-market fit and in your automated nurture campaigns, and move on. If you received the 'no' early on in your process, the prospect is showing you respect by not wasting your time.

"Your job is to go find the 'yes' as quickly as possible and let your automated marketing campaigns educate and nurture those 'not nows.' "

–Shannon Dolan, COO at Currence, Inc.

"I had the good fortune of going through the **Tafaro Growth Accelerator** program early in my career. As a young and malleable sales rep, I was able to see the direct results on revenue firsthand: more wins, faster wins, and larger contracts. It was so clear that this was the right way to do things.

"What I learned, however, is that this system requires two key components to succeed at every phase: An in-depth understanding of your customer's business needs (prospective or current), and a diligent buy-in to following a process.

"Each new hire joining a rapid scaling organization stressed this system. The overall firm expertise was diluted and adherence to following the process required more and more oversight. The process still worked, but the energy required to maintain the process scaled faster than the business.

"Much of this maintenance cost boiled down to an absence of technology to centralize, automate, and accelerate the deployment of this system—specifically in institutionalizing the understanding of customer business needs. Like the hub of a wheel, all other aspects of the system circled around understanding and communicating the value opportunity of how much you could improve a prospect's business or how well you were supporting a customer. The more clearly this was understood, the more easily and systematically each phase of the **Tafaro Growth Accelerator** could be deployed.

"What was continually shocking for me was the complete lack of technology in the marketplace that was built to understand and make sense of prospect needs and customer experience. Amidst a crowded landscape of sales, marketing, and account management tools, not one was focused on value for the business needs and experiences of their market.

"This gaping hole in the software landscape was the origin of building the B2B SaaS platform, Foresight. With the foundational principles of the **Tafaro Growth Accelerator** at its core, Foresight enables software businesses to capture value data at scale and put it into action.

"In the **Tafaro Growth Accelerator**, the Power Index is the method by which customer-facing teams engage their market. It's an incredibly powerful asset as it acts to both educate the market on the business needs that can and should be supported and provides an understanding of where current gaps exist. The challenges with the exercise lie in the difficulty of using it at scale without technology to support the design, distribution, and analysis of responses. Each step depends on manual effort.

"Foresight's platform is built around a *value assessment*, a technology enabled asset that takes the fundamentals of the Power Index to the next level and automates key phases of the sales process, distributing it to prospects and customers, analyzing the responses, and expanding on what it captures.

"Taking this a step further, using technology to automate this key aspect of the **Tafaro Growth Accelerator** unlocks a living, breathing understanding of market need. The data captured via *value assessments* creates an ever-building dataset of market insights.

"Foresight harnesses this data and reveals revenue-generating insights businesses have never had access to. For instance, how the needs of a company connect to the revenue outcome, how market needs are shifting over time, etc. This dataset stands to be a business's greatest asset as it contextualizes and informs all go-to-market activities across marketing, sales, account management, and product.

"Foresight's *value assessment*, when integrated with Steve's process, provides a system that integrates real-time, hyper-personalized insights into market needs that can feed every marketing campaign, conversation, sales process, and renewal. What felt like a far-off dream when first learning about the **Tafaro Growth Accelerator** is becoming a reality as more businesses can accelerate their growth trajectory by harnessing the power of great process and great technology."

–Nigel Hammond, cofounder at Foresight

Key Takeaways

- Alignment between sales and marketing means sharing strategy and goals that enable both groups to work together in a unified way.

- Your marketing messaging must arouse curiosity by showing prospects how others have benefited from your solution and how it can resolve the problems and issues they're dealing with.

- Buying is an emotional decision that prospects make after going through a rational product or service evaluation process. It is key that we influence that emotional decision.

- It's important to have a method to analyze the digital behavior of your targeted prospects and to score their behavior accordingly.

- Create separate campaigns for prospects your pre-sales team is nurturing to keep them engaged and aware of your activities in the market.

- The Power Index is a tool to uncover buyer needs. It lists all the capabilities or results a buyer can achieve by using your software and asks them to access whether they are underpowered or adequately powered in that specific application or functional area.

CHAPTER 5

BUILDING A SALES FOUNDATION

The *sales foundation* consists of the following four components:

1. The sales process.

2. The Power Index to uncover buyer needs and issues.

3. The Sales Productivity Index (SPI) to measure team and individual progress toward meeting performance goals.

4. Sales reporting and pipeline review.

1. The Sales Process

The **Tafaro Growth Accelerator** sales process includes a planned system of measurable and repeatable selling steps a salesperson is required to perform. The process consists of five phases: *Qualify, Verify, Position, Solve, and Confirm.*

Each phase incorporates selling steps and tactics that must be performed before moving a prospect to the next phase. By executing the process, salespeople will improve the accuracy, speed, and efficiency of the actions they can control. As they gain experience with the process, every interaction with a buyer will have greater impact and contribute to the objective of building long-term, profitable customers. These activities are based on scientific research about how people buy and how buyers mentally construct buying decisions.

In addition, productivity factors are established for each phase of the sales process and are consistently measured and evaluated. These include win rates by phase, the elapsed time to execute each phase, the average value of a sale, and the remaining months in the sales year. The productivity factors are used to produce the Sales Productivity Index (SPI) that will be presented later in this chapter.

It's important to emphasize that each phase within the sales process consists of a phase description, which is generic to the process. However, the specific selling activities that must be performed in each phase and the associated productivity factors can be different for each company. This should be configured based on your selling environment and how buying decisions are made. The specific selling activities and productivity factors shown in the book are examples of what you might configure for your company.

These are the objectives we're trying to achieve:

- Improve the sales win rate.
- Compress the sales cycle time.

- Eliminate "no decisions."

- Accurately forecast new business.

- Measure and improve the key criteria affecting sales performance.

The **Tafaro Growth Accelerator** sales process is built on the concept of value-based selling. It all starts with a discussion about a prospect's current situation and what they are trying to achieve. As discussed in **Principle Four:** *If buyers are either looking for a solution to a stated need, willing to discuss the fact that a problem exists, or admits dissatisfaction with a current situation, then a sale can potentially occur.* This leads us to **Principle Five:** *Value is defined as the economic benefit achieved by "closing the gap."*

The sales process is designed for salespeople to engage buyers (individual members of the buying team) through a rational process by helping them diagnose a specific problem or issue using the Power Index, and then work to determine what was causing it to exist.

Once buyers understand the impact of the problem and what caused it to exist, the salesperson can show the buyer how your software can solve the problem—or fill the gap. **Principle Six** states: *A solution emerges in the buyers' mind when they can visualize the actions that need to be taken to address their issues or solve their problems.* This rational approach will undoubtedly lead the buyer to their solution, but another principle comes into play here: **Principle Seven**: *Buyers buy what they need from people who understand what they want (the emotional component).*

A buyer is most likely to do business with the salesperson

who understands the buyer's personal needs based on their values, attitudes, and risk tolerance and/or need to succeed and enables the buyer to satisfy these needs. The most successful salespeople try to develop an interpersonal relationship with a buyer by taking an interest in what they are personally trying to achieve.

The flowing describes the five phases of the **Tafaro Growth Accelerator**. Remember, each phase description is generic to the process, but the specific activities that are required to be performed in each phase and the associated productivity factors must be configured.

Phase 1: QUALIFY

Phase Description: This phase is performed by a member of the pre-sales team whose job is to contact a prospective buyer who has shown interest in your software based on their digital behavior and has a high score in the lead scoring system, as discussed previously. At this point, the buyer can be anyone in a prospective account and is usually a mid-level executive or higher.

The purpose of the *Qualify* phase is to gain a general feeling of the prospect's interest in your software and their desire to learn more with the likelihood of advancing the sale. To accomplish this, the pre-salesperson should execute the appropriate "talk track" for the opportunity and either move the prospect to the *Verify* phase and facilitate a call with one of your sales representatives or place the prospect in the nurture category. If moved to nurture, pre-sales would schedule a follow-up time to either requalify or remove the prospect as warranting no future action.

Here is an example of an introductory "talk track":

Situation Analysis: You want to see if the prospect is curious, has been asked to evaluate solutions, or is actively looking. You also want to know who the *sponsoring executive* is behind the effort.

Talk Track and Questions
Thank him/her for their interest in our company and introduce yourself.

"My name is __________ and I am a solution consultant for __________. Thank you for your interest in our ____________. May I ask what prompted your interest in __________?"

Let the prospect talk!!!

"Is there someone in your org who is driving this interest?

<table>
<tr><td>

Anticipated Objections

Objections: We are just looking to see what is out there … (or) We're not actively looking.

Response: "*Great. What would you like to know about* _______________?"

Let the prospect talk and try to get him/her back into the verification process (see below).

Response: "*If I were to show you how we can help your firm generate a significant ROI from our solution, do you think your firm would be interested in understanding how we can solve some of the issues you are currently experiencing?*"

If no, "*Why don't I send you some information about* ____________ *and we'll stay in touch until you're actively looking.*"

If yes or maybe, "*We developed a Power Index that shows all the capabilities a firm like yours can have with* ____________. *I would like to send it to you and then schedule time to review it with you and to show you an overview of the system. How does that sound to you?*"

</td></tr>
</table>

Qualify Phase Productivity Factors

- Win rate (at conclusion of phase): 10%

- Time to complete the phase activities: 15 days

Phase Activities (conducted by pre-sales)

- Do your pre-call research about the prospect.

- Begin the talk track to identify the buyer's willingness to engage.

- Introduce the Power Index and ask permission to send it to the buyer.

- Explain the two-step sales process.

- Schedule a call with the buyer and a salesperson to review the Power Index and conduct an overview demo.

Questions to Answer

- What is the name and position of the buyer?

- Is this buyer interested in our solution?

- Is the buyer willing to participate in a call with our salesperson?

- Has the meeting date been confirmed?

- Where did the need originate in the organization?

Follow-up with the Prospect

- Email the buyer with the scheduled time for the sales meeting. Attach the Power Index and remind the buyer that our salesperson will be reviewing it when they meet.

- Label the prospect as a sales qualified lead (SQL) if a sales meeting has been scheduled. If not, place the prospect in nurture and schedule a follow-up call.

Phase 2: VERIFY

Verify Phase Productivity Factors

- Win rate (at conclusion of phase): 25%

- Time to complete the phase: 30 days

Phase Description: This is the phase that sets the engagement parameters. During the *Verify* phase, the salesperson should determine if the prospect is ready to engage in the sales process. **Principle Eight:** *If you decide to engage you must be able to eliminate a "no decision" result and have a reasonable chance of winning.*

This is a critical phase because of the elimination of a "no decision" outcome. The salesperson's initial discussion is with the buyer who has been contacted and qualified during pre-sales (initial buyer). It begins with a discussion about that buyer's current situation using the Power Index to determine where they may be "underpowered" and what they would like to achieve—from their point of view. Remember that different buyers have different needs, and it's not the product or service that wins the sale but the buyer's subjective view of what the product or service will do for them.

In working with our clients, we found that the following script works well because it simplifies the process in the buyer's mind. It goes like this: "We have a two-step process to help you evaluate our software. Step one is to show you an *overview demo* of our software to give you an idea of its look and feel, and then we review our Power Index for your area to understand how we can add value to your business. The Power Index will identify some of the issues you might be experiencing.

"In Step two we conduct a *working demo* to show you how our software addresses each issue, and together we work to establish the economic value of eliminating the issues that you identified. How does that sound?"[18]

The salesperson must impress the buyer and obtain

agreement to be introduced to other members of the buying team who will no doubt go through the same Power Index process. This is done through a series of questions that are part of the phase activities. Now is the time to begin to build rapport, establish your credentials, and develop a mutually agreeable plan of action.

Phase Activities

- Start by asking the buyer what he/she is trying to achieve via our discussions.

- Review the two-step process.

- Conduct the overview demo and Power Index review to determine areas of need.

- Schedule and conduct the working demo and value assessment. In most cases this is done on a subsequent call. The salesperson should give permission to invite others to be present for this session.

- Identify the *executive sponsor* and members of the buying team and use best practices for how to engage with them. The best question to ask is, "Besides yourself, who are the other folks that would be interested in seeing our software?"

- Agree on how/when the results of the working demo will be presented to other members of the buying team and the *executive sponsor*. The best follow-up question is, "If you're satisfied with the value we can provide for you, would you agree to introduce us to the others you previously mentioned?"

- Ask to understand the prospect's decision process.

- Confirm budget or access to funding.

Questions to Answer

- Is the prospect actively looking to change?

- Who is the *executive sponsor*?

- What is the prospect's decision-making process and when will a decision be made?

- Who are the members of the *buying team* and when can we have access to these members?

- Are funds available to license our solution or will funds need to be allocated?

Follow-up with Prospect

- Email initial buyer with mutually agreed plan of action.

Phase 3: POSITION

Position Phase Productivity Factors

Win rate (at conclusion of phase): 50%

Time to complete the phase: 45 days

Phase Description: In the *Position* phase the salesperson is engaging the relevant members of prospect's buying team, demonstrating your software by showing alternatives that address their issues and the gaps that were identified in the Power Index and establishing the economic value that can be delivered by "closing the gaps." Essentially, the salesperson is "positioning" key people within your company with their counterparts on the prospects buying team to create meaningful relationships.

Phase Activities

- Conduct working demo and Power Index value creation session/s with members of the buying team.

- Make sure to clearly understand the quantifiable value we can deliver from the prospect's perspective.

- Emphasize the competitive differentiation.

- Schedule a presentation to the *executive sponsor* and other relevant decision-makers.

- Present your company's competitive differentiators.

- Understand contract and legal review process.

Questions to Answer

- What is the quantifiable and specific value we will be delivering to the prospect?

- Does the prospect agree with this level of value?

- Have you established clear competitive differentiation?

- Do you have the agreement to present our value proposition to the *executive sponsor*?

- Have we confirmed the decision timeframe and budget?

- Who are our competitors?

Follow-up with Prospect

- Email everyone you've worked with explaining your next steps.

Phase 4: SOLVE

Solve Phase Productivity Factors

Win rate: 75%

Time to complete the phase: 30 days

Phase Description: At this point your salesperson has shown several members of the *buying team* how their needs can be addressed and how the economic value has been quantified. Now it's time to present to the *executive sponsor* and any remaining members of the *buying team* who are critical to winning. The objective is to solidify your solution and its inherent value, address any final questions, and submit a proposal to win the business.

Phase Activities

- Present results of the working demo and value assessment to the *executive sponsor* and relevant members of the *buying team*.

- Validate the value the prospect will receive.

- Clarify pricing and close any loose ends.

- Submit the final proposal.

- Agree on next steps with the executive sponsor.

Questions to Answer

- Have you presented the quantifiable and specific value we will be delivering to the buying team?

- Has the *executive sponsor* confirmed our value?

- Have we differentiated our value from the competition?

- Are there any critical decision-makers we have not engaged with?

- Have all issues been resolved?

Follow-up with Prospect

- Email the executive sponsor to confirm next steps.

Phase 5: CONFIRM

Confirm Phase Productivity Factors

Win rate: 95%

Time to complete the phase: 30 days

Phase Description: This is where we submit contracts, stay close to the prospect, and make sure we have active communications. Be aware of last-minute competitive actions.

Phase Activities

- Receive verbal notification.

- Reaffirm timeline, signatory, and steps needed.

- Resolve contract issues such as contract language and

security audits.

- Agree to timeline for execution.

- Monitor activities and maintain active communications.

Follow-up with Prospect

- Confirm receipt of agreements.

2. Sales Productivity Index (SPI)

To show the impact of a unified system, I would like to introduce a tool that I developed called the SPI—a foundational element of the **Tafaro Growth Accelerator**.

The SPI shows the importance of everything working together to achieve maximum performance. The SPI will enable you to track and measure sales productivity at both an individual and a team level. By comparing individual or team performance against the productivity factors that were established when the **Tafaro Growth Accelerator** was configured, the SPI will show the number of opportunities (by units and value) that are required in each phase of the sales pipeline, plus the times the pipeline must turn, to meet a sales objective (note that the number of times the pipeline should turn is based on the verify phase).

In addition, by comparing actual results (actual SPI) against the target SPI, individual and team performance can be measured, the areas requiring remediation can be improved, and the cost of noncompliance reduced.

Let's look at the various components of the sample SPI

below. It starts by looking at the remaining annual sales objective, the remaining months in the quota year, and the average value of a sale. These fields are entered by the salesperson and constantly change based on sales performance and elapsed time. In the beginning, the remaining annual sales objective is the salesperson's quota. But as deals are closed, that number decreases accordingly.

The next two sections show the five phases of the sales pipeline (*Qualify–Confirm*), the win rate by phase, and the average time to closure by phase. The fields in the Target column do not change, as they are the standards established when the productivity factors are configured. For example, the standards for the *Verify* phase indicate that a *Verified* opportunity has a 25% chance to close and is four months away from closure.

The fields in the Actual column represent the salesperson's actual performance. The salesperson's actual win rates and the number of months from closure are typically updated monthly based on actual performance. The compliance fields show how the salesperson complies with the standard.

Once all Actual fields are updated, the SPI will show the number of opportunities that are required to be in each phase of the pipeline and the number of times the pipeline must turn to meet quota. Turn is based on the *Verify* phase. For example, the SPI below shows seven accounts in *Verify*. Since a *Verified* opportunity is four months away from closing and has a win rate of 25%, the pipeline will have to turn twelve times for this salesperson to sell $1,250,000 of annual contracted revenue. Therefore, the salesperson will have to verify 84 opportunities through the first eight months of the year.

<table>
<tr><td colspan="4">Sales Productivity Index "SPI"</td></tr>
<tr><td>Remaining Annual Sales Objective</td><td>$1,250,000</td><td></td><td></td></tr>
<tr><td>Remaining Months In Year</td><td>12</td><td></td><td></td></tr>
<tr><td>Value of Average Sale</td><td>$60,000</td><td></td><td></td></tr>
</table>

Win Rate Percent by Phase	Target	Actual	Compliance
Qualify	10%	10%	100%
Verify	25%	25%	100%
Position	50%	50%	100%
Solve	75%	75%	100%
Confirm	95%	95%	100%

Average Time to Closure by Phase (months)	Target	Actual	Compliance
Qualify	5	5	100%
Verify	4	4	100%
Position	3	3	100%
Solve	2	2	100%
Confirm	1	1	100%

Pipeline Requirements	Phase	Deals	Dollars
	Qualify	17	$1,041,667
	Verify	7	$416,667

Position	3	$208,333
Solve	2	$138,889
Confirm	2	$109,649
Verify		
Turns	12	

Here are the Excel formulas for each phase:

Remaining Annual Sales Objective ÷ Value of the Average Sale ÷ Remaining Months in the Year ÷ Win Rate % (for the specific phase) ÷ Compliance % (for the specific phase) = the number of Opportunities for the phase.

Here are examples of questions to ask of salespeople that demonstrate how the SPI can be used in a coaching environment.[19]

Question #1

Based on the productivity factors in the SPI above how many opportunities would I need in the *Verify* phase if my win rate was 30% instead of 25%?

Answer

- With a higher win rate, I would only need six opportunities in *Verify*.

Question #2

What would my actual SPI be if my time to closure was one month longer for the first three phases of the pipeline per pipeline phase?

Answer

Pipeline Phases	Original Units Required per Phase	New Units Required by Phase	Cost of Non-Compliance (Units)	Cost of Non-Compliance (Dollars)
Qualify	17	21	4	$240,000
Verify	7	9	1	$120,000
Position	3	5	2	$120,000

Question #3

What would my actual SPI be for each phase if the value of the average sale was $50,000 instead of $60,000?

Pipeline Phases	Units at $60,000	Units at $50,000	Cost of Non-Compliance (Units)
Qualify	17	21	4
Verify	7	8	1
Position	3	4	1
Solve	2	3	1
Confirm	2	2	0

Question #4

What would my SPI look like going into month three if I didn't sell anything in the first two months?

Pipeline Phases	Original SPI	New SPI	Cost of Non-Compliance (Units)
Qualify	17	21	2
Verify	7	8	1
Position	3	4	1
Solve	2	3	1
Confirm	2	2	0

3. Sales Reporting and Pipeline Review Process

It is extremely important to have timely and accurate sales reporting to assess how every pre-sales and salesperson is progressing toward achieving their performance objectives. The following information should be kept current rather than being updated monthly. It is necessary to see where everyone is on a virtual basis. It's not about what happened last month—the focus should be on what is happening now to effect change.

Pre-Sales Virtual Reporting

- # of leads you're trying to contact (sorted by lead scoring)

- # of leads that have been contacted

- # of leads that entered the *Qualify* phase

- # of leads you've *Qualified*

- # of leads in the nurture phase

Sales Virtual Reporting

- Quota ACV (annual contract value)

- Sold ACV

- % of quota

- Number of deals closed

- Average ACV

- Current SPI

Sales leaders were required to conduct coaching sessions with each salesperson on their team every two weeks to review sales progress and pipeline activity. The purpose of the coaching sessions is to understand what each salesperson needs to do to meet target objectives, identify areas requiring remediation, and offer guidance on the strategy and tactics necessary to take each prospect through the phases of the sales process. A typical coaching session would follow this agenda:

1. Review the virtual sales report to identify the salesperson's current position relative to quota attainment.

2. Each salesperson presents their SPI and identifies areas of noncompliance. These could be related to the number and value of the opportunities in the pipeline or the elapsed time per phase.

3. Discuss what needs to be done to close all opportunities in the Solve and *Confirm* phases and develop an action plan for each prospect.

4. Review the deals in the *Qualify* phase to see the number of leads entering the pipeline. This is critical to avoid hills and valleys in performance. If there is an inadequate number of leads entering the pipeline, the pre-sales team should be notified, and efforts should be made to the work with the salespeople who need more *Qualify* opportunities.

5. The last area of focus is the opportunities in *Verify* and *Position*. These are the two most difficult phases for salespeople to execute. You will find that some salespeople will rely on old behaviors, find it difficult to ask the right questions, and often miss a step or two in executing the phase activities. This is where coaching can be most helpful, but it will require patience from the sales leaders. The key lesson here is for the sales leader to demand mastery of these two phases. In time, sales performance will greatly improve.

    Initially, it's necessary to conduct these sessions every two weeks to change behavior and get every salesperson proficient in executing the sales process versus doing their own thing. Later, formal coaching sessions can be scheduled monthly along with informal meetings to discuss strategy about individual deals scheduled as needed.

Comments from the Experts

"Steve's (Sales Foundations) program ensured us that we had a tight alliance between sales and marketing and allowed for the flexibility to adjust as needed. Adherence to Steve's planning through utilization of both the Power Index and the **Tafaro Growth Accelerator** process to manage opportunities based on preset criteria within each stage of an opportunity helped us ensure success. In addition, the SPI enabled us to gain efficiency by improving win rates and compressing the sales cycle. I found his system easy to implement and use while being extremely effective. It also enabled us to build a repeatable and scalable process that helped train both new sales and business development."

–Bob Laurenzo, VP of sales at Gotham Tech Group

"We incorporated Steve's selling system back in 2016 when DealCloud was an emerging company. His methods delivered aggressive growth and market leading outcomes in a highly competitive marketplace. Having used the **Tafaro Growth Accelerator** system for over seven years, I have found the following adjustments to be extremely helpful. In addition to eliminating a 'no decision' outcome in the *Verify* phase, I encouraged my team to ask the tough questions early in the phase to determine whether we should continue engaging or move the prospect to the nurture category. It is important to understand whether the prospect is in the education or buying stage. Our productivity increased by compressing the amount of time we spent with each prospect in *Verify* simply by making this determination. I found the Power Index to be a very useful tool because it solidified the pain points and identified areas for improvement from the prospect's perspective and enables us to develop a compelling and meaningful ROI. In addition to identifying the *executive sponsor* in the *Verify* phase, we encouraged our salespeople to understand who must see the software to approve a transaction. In addition to the users, there are often buyers in IT, purchasing, operations, etc. who need to be involved. It is important to identify these folks early on.

"At the conclusion of the *Position* phase, we emphasized the need for a communication cadence to hold both parties accountable as we progressed forward with the sale. The SPI is critical for understanding any gaps that need to be filled in the target pipeline. This is a great way for both sales and marketing to align on how they view the pipeline. How much is there in each phase? Does that give us what we need to successfully hit the target or is there a gap? Where should we focus the pre-sales team, etc.?"

–Michael Santos, VP of sales at DealCloud, Inc.

"Steve is a boundless source of energy, enthusiasm, and experience. I had the privilege of learning from Steve early in my career and have taken his methods and systems with me to each of my next opportunities—SPI in particular. As you implement the recommendations, imagine a coach sitting beside you with passion, command of craft, sense of urgency, and the ability to communicate while willing you to succeed, making you want to be accountable to him and yourself. The act of creating this book demonstrates Steve's inherited generosity and his way of scaling himself so that you too can be successful.

"I cannot express how effective implementing and refining the SPI can be for creating a culture of accountability, performance, and success. The insights you gain as you work the SPI model feeds back to product, support, marketing, and leadership. The process and supporting tools like the Power Index, expertly crafted scripts, and questionnaires will provide insights that you can tweak and tack to hone your sales process, technical product, and service deliverables—and this feedback comes direct from the clients and prospects.

"There are so many lessons in this chapter, like validating decision-makers. In the sample talk track, one of Steve's qualifying questions is, 'Is there someone in your organization who is driving this interest?' This question is important at every stage, but perhaps worded in slightly different ways. With each interaction, you want to confirm that you understand the path to closure, and who on the prospect side is key to that decision; the influencers, the actual decision-makers, and the process they need to go through to make the decision. This information is vitally important to effectively forecast the close, which is a big part of a sales team's responsibility to accurately forecast the amount and timing of the pipe.

"In stage three, Steve addresses demonstrating your solution. When Steve and I were first working together, we targeted a complex accounting solution for the private equity market. There were many screens, a lot of data fields, reporting, and automation. This made the demo long and with many clicks, which did not effectively portray the power and efficiency gained from implementing the solution. We worked with a professional demo agency to fine-tune our demo methods. We did not just show up and 'throw up.' The only thing worse than sitting through an hour-long feature-focused demo with no tie back to my problems or challenges is when it lasts longer than an hour. Invest in your demo approach, vary it up with recordings, live in-product components, and always tie back to the Power Index, which focuses on the problems you have agreed with the prospect they are expecting your solution to solve.

"Finally, I'd say the most important thing to understand as you work through the sales foundation and implement the SPI is that you are taking control of the sales process. You are establishing your confirmed path to successful sales and overall relationship. You are setting the right expectations for both the pre- and post-sale relationship. An effective sales process leads to smooth implementations, high client satisfaction, and high client retention. Don't let your prospects run your process—it is inefficient and introduces risk to a successful outcome in the near term and over the life of the client relationship. Run your process."

–Shannon Dolan, COO at Currence, Inc.

Key Takeaways

- The **Tafaro Growth Accelerator** sales process is built on the concept of value-based selling.

- There are five phases to the process. Each phase includes selling steps and tactics that must be performed before moving a prospect to the next phase.

- A sale can occur if buyers agree that there is a discrepancy or gap between their "current state" and "where they want to be." Value is defined as the economic benefit of "closing the gap."

- The Sales Productivity Index (SPI) is a foundational element to the process that will enable you to track and measure sales productivity at both an individual and team level.

- Regularly scheduled coaching sessions with each

individual should be designed to change sales behavior by identifying areas requiring remediation and offering guidance on the strategy and tactics necessary to take each prospect through the phases of the sales process.

CHAPTER 6

DEVELOPING AN ACCOUNT MANAGEMENT FOUNDATION

Recurring revenue (RR) is the engine that drives value in a SaaS software business. New accounts, higher pricing, lower churn, and upsells all contribute to RR.

A good question to ask yourself is, "If we were to shut down our new account sales team tomorrow and held our existing accounts at a steady state, what would the company look like a year from now?" With exceptional account management, it would grow organically. That's the beauty of SaaS.

Account managers are the link to organic growth, and that's why I recommend they be organized as a self-contained unit separate from your new account sales team. Account managers draw upon a broad skill set that involves both planning and execution. As planners, they need to consider the entire account landscape, understand the various stakeholders, identify potential areas where additional services could provide added value, and construct an account growth plan aimed at expanding the user base and introducing new applications.

From an execution standpoint, they should be adept at using their domain knowledge to facilitate the resolution of technical and user issues. The growth plan should also be implemented while building trust and interpersonal relationships with the members of the *buying team* in their respective accounts. Effective account management will reduce the churn rate and maximize lifetime value.

Account management begins with implementation and the onboarding and initial roll-out of your software. This is the one area in which your company will immediately be tested, and how you respond can set the tone for your account relationship going forward. If a customer's initial experience with your software and/or your company's response during onboarding and roll-out does not meet their expectations, you're setting the stage for potential churn.

On the other hand, if they're satisfied with the effort, their confidence increases, and the stage is set for a long-term relationship. This is what makes this such a critical period. If technical folks or product specialists are required for data integration, configuration, or to help the customer make decisions as to how to best deploy your software to further develop their business, account managers should facilitate the process and be viewed by the customer as serving their interests.

Even after implementation, there will be times when

users need the help of technical resources to fix glitches or interface problems. Account managers must take an active role in the process until issues are resolved. For this reason, your account managers must be the face of your company during this time. Retaining customers starts with delivering value and support when they most need it.

Ultimately, account management is largely about nurturing relationships. This requires an intimate understanding of the needs, wants, budget constraints, and communication preferences of the users they serve to create long-lasting relationships. Without an understanding of how users view and interact with your product, how can you know what's working and what isn't?

Once a relationship of trust is formed with their current users, account managers should have a plan to connect with others. This is best done by mapping the account to identify other key players that interface with or use your software, which includes other users, technical staff, operations, and at least one executive sponsor.

A good way to expand relationships is to take a consultative approach by making every effort to connect with users to understand their needs and problems. Present ideas on how to improve user experience and value. Focus on streamlining workflows and minimizing superfluous options, and use the Power Index as a tool to identify issues other users have that can be addressed through your software.

Account Planning

Account planning is the process of building strategic and tactical plans that foster value-driven relationships with your customers. It's also a time management tool that helps account managers focus their efforts on those customers who are either experiencing issues and those that have the best opportunity for growth. Without effective account planning it's difficult to achieve the results and outcomes your company and customers are looking for—all of which will increase the lifetime value to your business.

Account planning starts with account segmentation. Not every account is in the same position regarding the use of your software, and this position will change over time. Some will have immediate issues that have to be addressed while others will be primed for growth.

The three basic segmentation categories are:

- **Growth mode**: These are the accounts that have the potential to increase your revenue and grow your relationship. A strategic plan will be required to maximize growth opportunity.

- **Troubled mode**: Accounts in troubled mode typically deal with issues that must be addressed because they could negatively impact your long-term relationship or become candidates for churn. These accounts require immediate action.

- **Stable mode**: Customers in this category are generally pleased with your software and are happy with the status quo.

Remember, these categories represent the current position of each account. So, if I had 10 accounts in each position, I would first focus my time on resolving the issues with those customers in troubled mode and immediately start constructing plans to maximize the opportunities with those customers in growth mode. The enemy of account management is time, and this segmentation process enables account managers to invest time for maximum results.

We previously addressed the role of the account manager as facilitator with those customers in troubled mode, but what about those in growth mode? Here's an account growth process that's a modified version of the **Tafaro Growth Accelerator** and has proven to be successful with many of my clients.

Account Growth Process

The account growth process employs similar phases to the **Tafaro Growth Accelerator** sales process and is designed to obtain buy-in from account leaders to implement a mutually beneficial growth plan consisting of upselling and cross-selling activities. These are tactics that account managers can use to sell more and increase the stickiness of your relationship. When you're upselling, you're convincing account leadership to expand the usage of what they've already licensed. This could be licensing additional seats, implementing other user groups, or upgrading the current version of your software. Cross-selling involves licensing complementary applications that integrate with those already installed.

The account growth process features activities that account managers need to execute that are designed to improve the quality, speed, and efficiency of the actions they can control, and thereby influence end results. The process has five phases: *Qualify, Verify, Position, Solve and Confirm.*

Phase 1: QUALIFY

The purpose of the *Qualify* phase is for account managers to identify those accounts in growth mode that have a good chance of increasing annual recurring revenue (ARR) via upselling or cross-selling. These will be considered *qualified accounts*. Once identified, each account manager should record the following information.

Phase Activities

- Account name

- Leadership team: Defined as the person/s responsible for implementing your software, your primary user (our champion/s), and the *executive sponsor* (COO, CTO, CFO etc.).

- Our current position: Number of users, user groups, applications installed, etc.

- Customer's growth objectives: Relative to your software.

- Opportunity: Other applications (cross-selling) and/ or user groups (upselling), etc. that will help the leadership team achieve its objectives while maximizing the usage of your software.

- Projected annual recurring revenue (ARR) for the specific opportunity.

Phase 2: VERIFY

The purpose of the *Verify* phase is to get agreement from a qualified account's *executive sponsor* to move forward with a mutually developed growth plan. This is best achieved through the following actions:

Phase Activities

- Review both the account's growth objectives and your objectives with your champion/s.

- Construct a roadmap of cross-selling or upselling activities with your champion/s designed to meet mutual growth objectives.

- Present the roadmap to the *executive sponsor* and obtain agreement to introduce it to additional user groups within the account.

- Ask the *executive sponsor* to introduce you to the additional targeted users.

- Project the ARR for the proposed cross-selling or upselling opportunities in the road map.

Once the account manager has executive agreement, the account is verified, and the progress reviewed with management is similar to reviewing a sales pipeline.

Phase 3: POSITION

The *Position* phase consists of meetings with target user groups to explore specific upsell and cross-sell activities in the plan.

Phase Activities

- Meet with each user group leveraging the suggestion of the *executive sponsor*.

- Use the Power Index to surface user needs (gaps) for upselling or cross-selling opportunities.

- Demonstrate how your software can address the needs and jointly develop the potential value of closing the gaps.

- Update the ARR for the opportunities in position.

Phase 4: SOLVE

The *Solve* phase consists of presenting the potential value that was developed with each user group back to the *executive sponsor*. When cross-selling, be sure to identify the added value derived from the flow of information of integrated applications, and how the added information can affect decision-making.

Phase Activities

- Present the proposed value to the *executive sponsor*.

- Get agreement to submit a proposal. Clarify pricing and close any loose ends. Agree on next steps with the *executive sponsor*.

- Update the ARR for the opportunities being proposed.

Phase 5: CONFIRM

In the *Confirm* phase, you're finalizing the agreement in order to proceed.

Phase Activities

- Receive verbal notification.

- Reaffirm timeline, signatory, and steps needed.

- Resolve contract issues.

Account Growth Coaching and Reporting

Typically, account managers will need ongoing coaching to help resolve internal and external issues and obstacles preventing them from advancing from their current position. Process review and strategy sessions should be scheduled at least every two weeks between account management and each account manager. Each account manager should present the following information in each phase of the account growth process:

- Name of the account.

- Cross-selling and upselling opportunities.

- Number of days that each opportunity has been in the specific phase.

- Updated ARR.

Comments from the Experts

"Steve is passionate about clarity and definition of role, especially the difference between new sales and account management, as am I. My experience is, without that clarity of role, it's easy to get distracted and lose sight of the priorities as you deal with the challenges of the moment. To achieve high growth, the team focused on new sales needs to be measured and compensated differently than those focused on account management. Both are extremely important.

"Leadership sometimes does not really appreciate the value of an account management team or sees that function as less important. I encourage you to understand the cost of new customer acquisition if that thought ever crosses your mind. If you have a leaky bucket, you are essentially paying twice for that same dollar of revenue. That's a waste of time and resources, both of which are scarce and critical when in high growth.

"I disagree with Steve slightly, as I believe in early stage and start-up phases the same person can and often does perform both functions. However, it is critically important for that person to understand when they are switching hats and actively lean into the different skills and competencies needed to be successful in each role. As soon as growth allows, separating the functions will be key to accelerated growth. Watching leading indicators like support tickets, mean time to resolution, customer satisfaction surveys, social posts, app store comments, and ratings along with daily, weekly, monthly analysis of attrition data will let you know if separating the functions needs to move up the priority list."

—Shannon Dolan, COO at Currence, Inc.

Key Takeaways

- Recurring revenue (RR) is the engine that drives value in a SaaS software business. New accounts, higher pricing, lower churn, and upsells all contribute to RR.

- Account managers are the link to organic growth

and draw upon a broad skill set that involves both planning and execution.

- Account planning is the process of building strategic and tactical plans that foster value-driven relationships with your customers.

- If a customer's experience with your company's response during onboarding and roll-out or when there are software issues that need to be resolved does not meet their expectations, you're setting the stage for potential churn. On the other hand, if they're satisfied with the effort, their confidence increases, and the stage is set for a long-term relationship.

- A good way to expand relationships is to take a consultative approach by making every effort to connect with users to understand their needs and problems and then present ideas on how to improve user experience and value.

- Without effective account planning, it's difficult to achieve the results and outcomes your company and your customers are looking for—all of which will increase their lifetime value to your business.

CONCLUSION

*W*inning at SaaS is the playbook I've helped SaaS companies follow to sustainable growth and life-changing success. I hope you find it to be a valuable resource as you create the sales and marketing foundations, tools, and skills that will enable your company to accelerate growth and shareholder value.

As I stated in the introduction, success today is based on months, not years. It requires exceptional leadership, a customer-centric culture, and a logical, measurable, and repeatable sales process that's flawlessly executed. You'll also need an organization that's aligned and committed to winning new business, maintaining the highest degree of customer satisfaction, and continuously adding value.

Leadership, Culture, Execution, and Alignment

- **Leadership**: Leading a sales and marketing organization is much different than managing one because leadership is all about people. You can only lead people—people in sales, account management, and marketing that have been inspired by your vision and your ability to effectively communicate it. Work with them, teach them, and coach them. Enable them to participate in designing and building your vision and your processes. If you do, they will not let you down.

- **Culture**: Remember that your long-term success, especially in the SaaS model, will be dependent on your customers' success. Winning must be mutual and based on creating value. This means that you first must understand what the customer is trying to achieve, identify their issues, and then work together on solutions that address them. Creating a culture based on offering continuous value will drive organic growth.

- **Execution**: The ability to execute the phases in any sales process demands that you provide consistent coaching, identify areas requiring remediation, and collaborate on strategy and tactics to produce a win-win result. Remember that you're changing behavior from the old ways of selling to a customer-centric approach, and this necessitates practice and repetition.

- **Alignment**: *Winning at SaaS* is built around the core belief that sales and marketing are two sides of the same coin and must be viewed as a unified process in which strategy and tactics are aligned within the company. Alignment around a shared vision and constant communication among your marketing, sales, and account management teams is critical to success and to overcoming challenges.

There is an old saying: "Luck is where preparation meets opportunity." *Winning at SaaS* will prepare your go-to-market professionals to meet their opportunities with confidence. The foundations, tools, and skills presented in the **Tafaro Growth Accelerator** will make your sales and marketing team your greatest asset. If you follow the recommendations in this playbook, everyone involved will learn to execute the strategies and techniques necessary to build strong relationships with today's buyers that give them the peace of mind and confidence to choose you.

RESOURCES AND LEARNING

The following appendices present a library of situational skills and techniques that everyone engaging with prospects and customers will need to master.

We use the term *buying team* because buying decisions are rarely made by one individual. The people making buying decisions are often present throughout the organization and may vary from sale to sale. Some of the members of the buying team may consult with others (both inside and outside of the organization) who can help influence the buying decision.

In every sale, members of the buying team will perform three basic buying functions before a buying decision can be made. Below we will explore the typical members of the buying team, the buying functions, and how influence can affect a buying decision.

The Buying Team

- **Decision-maker(s):** This executive (or group) has formal authority and responsibility for the business initiative and its funding.

- **Approver:** This executive will support recommendations from the *executive sponsor* and buying team, approve the buying decision, and recommend to the decision-maker/s that funds be committed.

- **Evaluators**: These are the people who will evaluate how your software performs and its ability to meet business and technical specifications.

- **Executive sponsor:** This is the executive who will ultimately own the solution, its roll-out, and results. This individual will have the most to gain or lose from the business decision. In some cases, the *executive* sponsor is also the approver. In any case, this is the person we must win over.

The Three Buying Functions:

1. Facilitating

Someone within the organization will be responsible for facilitating the buying activities. This is usually one of the first buyers with whom we have contact. This person could come from purchasing, the technical area, or the user community. Their role is to gather information, do some initial screening about the vendor's ability to meet certain specifications, and facilitate the buying process. This individual is most often not a decision-maker but can block us from access to the buying team. Our objective is to effectively navigate from this individual to the key members of the buying team.

2. Performance and Technology Assessment

This role is performed by people within the buying organization who will be users of your software, and their objective is to evaluate how your software will perform.

Performance can be based on meeting business needs or to evaluate whether your software meets certain technical specifications—usually around integration and security.

3. Recommending and Funding

Once selected, it must be recommended to the decision-maker/s and approved as a budgetary expense. This role may be performed by one or more people.

The Importance of Influence

There are certain individuals whose opinions count. These are people who may not be in positions of authority but have earned a degree of power and influence within an organization based on their past contributions. There are others who reside outside of an organization but have contributed value in the past and are often consulted before important decisions are made. They may also be users of our solution in "like businesses" who can influence members of the buying team. In any case, these influencers can affect the outcome of a deal and must be part of a winning strategy.

As we search for potential influencers, we should look inside and outside of the organization. LinkedIn is a great tool for finding potential outside influencers. Researching the relationships and contacts members of the buying team have with executives in like businesses, advisors, legal counselors, and consultants will enable you to find referral sources who can recommend our solution and company, thereby mitigating buying risk.

As we look inside the organization, we want to identify

those individuals who have contributed value in the past, may be connected to key executives on the buying team, and who are relied upon to help create the vision and direction for the organization.

APPENDIX B:
EXECUTIVE BUYER CONVERSATIONS

n many cases you will be selling to several types of buyers within an organization. When doing so, it's important to remember that they will be considering your solution from their business's point of view.

Users are interested in the features and benefits that make their life easier. Middle managers will focus on how your solution can help solve some of the issues they're dealing with and help them meet the objectives imposed on them by senior management.

When you sell to individuals at these levels, you will face more competition, be treated as a commodity, and constantly deal with pricing issues. However, if you can relate your solution to the mindset of the executive buyers, you will have less competition, be considered more of a strategic partner, and face fewer price issues.

Executive buyers will focus on more strategic organizational issues such as revenue growth, market share, profit, and competitive positioning. Often, you must navigate from the middle managers to the executive buyer.

To effectively sell to executive buyers, it's important to understand the key issues they face, know what they look for to gain trust in a sales executive or account manager, and properly prepare for the conversation.

The Key Issues of Different Executive Buyers

Different executives have different key issues. The chart below is an example of issues most relevant to the CEO, CFO, and CIO:

Chief Executive CEO	Chief Financial Officer CFO	Chief Information Officer CIO
• Customer loyalty • Organizational culture and alignment • Increasing market share • Hiring, developing, and retaining skilled employees • Productivity improvements	• Optimizing financial metrics • Reducing costs by maximizing efficiency • Improving the return on human capital • Maximizing the return on investments and on the company's assets	• Effectively deploying technology • Security • Leveraging knowledge management • Intellectual property protection • Maximizing scalability and compatibility

Source: Nicholas A.C. Read and Stephen J. Bistritz, *Selling to the C-Suite: What Every Executive Wants You to Know About Successfully Selling to the Top* (New York: McGraw-Hill, 2009).

What Executive Buyers Expect
of Sales Executives

- Here are five traits that executives expect from the salespeople and account managers they engage with:

  o Have knowledge of their industry and their company strategy.

  o First understand their issues and then offer solutions that create value.

  o Be consistent, dependable, and demonstrate integrity.

  o Act like you are entering a long-term partnership rather than pursuing a single sale.

  o Have the ability and authority to marshal the resources needed to address key problems and issues that may develop.

Mastering these will build credibility and trust with C-level executives.

APPENDIX C:
VALUE-BASED SELLING

For salespeople and account managers to succeed, they must first understand the issues and concerns of the business executives they're calling on, and then be highly skilled at creating value by presenting solutions to address these issues and concerns.

Value-Based Selling

Value-based selling starts with understanding buyers' needs and what they're trying to achieve from their point of view. Remember that different buyers have different needs. Your objective is to help buyers close the gap that exists between where their organization is today and where they need to be.

If buyers are either looking for a solution to a stated need or willing to discuss the fact that a problem exists, then a sale can potentially occur. Buyers must agree that there's a discrepancy or gap between their current state and where they want to be. Value is defined as the economic benefit achieved by closing the gap.

You must first take the buyers through a rational process by helping them diagnose the problem. Only then can you work to determine what's causing it to exist. Once buyers understand the impact of the problem and what's causing it to exist, you can then facilitate a process of exploring various options to solve the problem—or fill the gap. A "solution image" occurs when the buyers can visualize the actions that need to be taken to address their need or solve their problem (use the Power Index described in the book as the tool to uncover issues and problems buyers are dealing with).

Good questioning will help create a dialogue that will assist in visualizing the image of the solution we're proposing. Here are a few questions to consider:

- How did you do it today?

- What issues are you experiencing?

- What would the right solution allow you to do?

- What would be the economic benefit of this solution?

In demonstrating a product or service, relate it to the solution image you've helped to create. This should be done in bits and pieces by showing each solution area and discussing its relevant value. It will also be important to differentiate the solution from competitors. Most often, people decide by differentiating. If you don't create a distinction, the buyer will create one on their own.

The best way to summarize the process is to create a value statement. This is best done together with the *executive sponsor*. A value statement includes the following:

Through a working demo you indicated that
your firm was underpowered in the following

*areas: (list each area). We showed how our
solution will enable you to (describe what our
solution will enable the prospect to achieve for
each area). Together we estimated the financial impact of this capability to be (describe
the quantitative and qualitive value for each
area). This will require an annual investment
of (the annual cost of our solution), which will
be returned within (the timeframe for return
in months).*

If you follow this process diligently, you will be in a much stronger position to influence end results.

One of the best books about selling is *Conceptual Selling*, written by Robert Miller and Stephen Heiman in 1989. In the book, the authors refer to work done by psychologist J.P. Guilford in 1960 that very much applies to decision-making today. Guilford suggests that in making rational decisions people use different types of thinking. Among those that are the most important are cognition, divergence, and convergence, and rational decisioning always puts these three types in the same order.[20]

- **Cognitive thinking**: Buyers seek to understand the situation. It gives buyers the information they need to know where they are and what kind of problem they are facing. Cognitive thinking doesn't seek solutions; it merely provides a fix on the current situation.

- **Divergent thinking:** Buyers will consider alternatives. This type of thinking allows the buyers to survey various solutions that may be available.

- **Convergent thinking:** Buyers make the decision. Having surveyed their options, buyers converge on the solution they deem to be the best.

Miller and Heiman emphasize the importance of understanding that this type of thinking happens in a flow of thought rather than in distinct phases. Most of the time is spent assessing the situation. If you disrupt the natural flow of the thinking process by trying to move the buyer to convergence without allowing him or her to work through cognition and divergence, this ignores the buyer's "concept" and deprives the buyer of choice.

Buyers love to buy, but they hate the feeling that they have been sold. Buyers therefore become confused, angry, and resistant. Through proper questioning, you can help the buyers to process information, show them the alternatives, and provide them with a better way to verbalize what they are seeking.

Most buying decisions are based on need. If the buyer is willing to discuss the fact that a potential problem may exist or admits dissatisfaction with the current situation, a sale can potentially occur. Your role then becomes helping the buyer identify a solution image. A solution image occurs when the buyer can visualize the actions that need to be taken to achieve their goal.

No two buyers buy the same product or service for precisely the same reasons. It's not the product or service that breaks the sale but the buyer's subjective view of what the product or service will do for them.

Here is a flow of questioning to illustrate the learning points above:

- How do you accomplish this today?

- What are the issues with your current way of addressing the situation?

- What's the impact on your business?

- What if you could …?

- Can I show you how others have dealt with this situation?

- Can you see the benefit of this approach versus your current approach?

- How would this impact your organization?"

- What does better look like to you?"

There's one additional and significant point. Any accomplished account manager can execute the concepts above, but the great ones understand that the ultimate buying decision is a personal and emotional one.

The rational process above will lead the buyer to their solution image. However, the buyer will do business with the individual who understands that the buyer also has personal needs that must be met (based on values, attitudes, risk tolerance and/or need to succeed) and enables the buyer to satisfy these needs.

APPENDIX E:
THE OVERVIEW DEMO AND THE WORKING DEMO

It's important to remember that a product demonstration (demo) given to a buyer is essentially an extension of the sales engagement. If the following activities are conducted properly with the right individual(s), the effectiveness of the demo itself will be greatly enhanced.

Do Your Research

Prior to scheduling the demo, you should gather information about the prospect and references of people they know or like firms that have gained value from your software.

Align With the Decision-Makers

It is important to make sure that you identify the individual's title and responsibility. If the demo is scheduled in advance, be sure you know who will participate and know their titles and responsibilities. Discuss this with the facilitator in advance.

Conduct the Overview Demo
and Power Index Review

The *overview demo* is given to show a member of the buying team a high-level overview of your software and is accompanied by a needs analysis exercise using the Power Index. There is a script that I recommend when meeting a new buyer. It goes like this:

"We have a two-step process to help you evaluate our software. Step one is to show you an overview of our software to give you an idea of its look and feel, and then we review our Power Index for your area to understand how we can add value to your business. The Power Index will identify some of the issues you might be experiencing. In step two, we conduct a *working demo* to show you how our software addresses each issue, and together we work to establish the value of addressing the issues that arise."

The idea is to get buyers excited to the point where they agree to schedule a *working demo*. When presenting the overview demo, explain the key areas of functionality they will see and try to present a use case for each area. After seeing the overview demo, introduce the Power Index as a tool we use to uncover the issues the buyer may be experiencing. Remember that some of their issues can be latent—they may not be able to articulate what they need. Many times, people are dealing with issues and are unaware that a solution exists.

Conducting the Working Demo

If there are multiple participants, take the lead by introducing yourself and your role. Ask the buyer you have been working with to introduce the participants to their side. As folks are introduced, make sure you understand their roles within the firm. Remember to engage the buyers and get them to talk about their situation as much as possible.

Review the highlights of the Power Index with the buyers by emphasizing the issues that were uncovered and where they are underpowered. Get everyone's acknowledgement of the issues.

General Demo Instructions

Introduce the demo by explaining what you will be showing the buyers to give them a feel for the components, functionality, and flow of the demo. This should only take 10 minutes or so. Explain that this is a *working demo.* Its purpose is to address their issues and areas where they are underpowered, show how your software can address the issues, and discuss the economic benefit that can be achieved by eliminating the issues.

Introduce each area of functionality and confirm where they are underpowered. Show how your solution addresses each one, or how like firms used the system accordingly. Have dialogue with the prospect about it and get their agreement that we can address the issue.

Ask what it would mean if this issue was resolved. This is the key question for the cost/benefit analysis. Repeat this process for each key underpowered area. Summarize by reviewing what they've seen, gain acknowledgement of the issues that we have addressed, and ask if there is anything else we can show them.

Agree on a specific plan of action going forward.

Demo Follow-up

Email the participants and thank them for their atten-dance and interest. Summarize the highlights of the demo and layout of the plan of action discussed.

Here is a list of FAQs that everyone who touches the customer should be familiar with.

Company

How long have you been around?

How many total clients do you have?

Who are your investors?

Who is on the board?

How many employees do you have?

Are you profitable?

What is your retention rate?

What is your churn?

What are your weaknesses?

Who is your main competition?

How do I know you will be around in five years?

Platform

What is your technology built on?

Do you integrate with other solutions?

Do you have a mobile app?

Is the system configurable?

Can we install this locally?

Can you permission users?

Do you have an open API?

Do you work on all operating systems?

Implementation and Support

How long does implementation take?

How involved does our team have to be during the implementation process?

What is your support model?

Do you have an account management team?

Do you have 24/7 support?

How do you support clients in different time zones?

Can your team make suggestions on best practices?

Where is your implementation team located?

Will you upload our data?

Will I have an account manager?

Will we be able to design our own reports? Can you do that for us?

Security

How do you ensure our data is secure?

Will you have visibility into our data?

What happens to our data if we decide to cancel a subscription?

Where are your servers located?

Will our data be secure from your other clients?

What is your disaster recovery process?

Do you have two-factor authentication?

Do you run security audits?

Are you SOC compliant?

Financial

Do you have an implementation fee?

When do we have to start paying?

Does your mobile application cost extra?

What is your cancellation policy?

What is the length of the contract?

Is it auto renewable?

Is there a fee for additional training or for using your support team?

Can I get a free trial?

As you build your SaaS business you may need to raise equity capital for growth and expansion. Egis Capital Partners is a private equity firm located in New Jersey focused on the security and protection industry. The firm is led by Robert Chefitz, a 36-year veteran of the private equity industry.

Mr. Chefitz felt that his firm needed a common language around risk when looking at a specific investment and that the eight categories below would ensure a thoughtful discussion. The sub-points under each category further define that area of risk and are meant to be discussed when assessing the specific category. Each sub-point is scored from 1 to 10 to capture the magnitude of risk, with 10 being the lowest risk and 1 being the highest risk.

Opportunity

1. Management Risk
• Experience of the team
• Entrepreneurial drive and spirit
• Domain knowledge
• Team working together
• Business leadership
• Level of comparable achievement
• Ability to recruit first-class management team
• Ability to hire required personnel
2. Business Model
• Historical performance
• Cost, margins, and returns
• Pricing knowledge
• Customer acceptance
• Sales cycle
• Distribution
• Capital required
• Regulatory issues
3. Competitive Risk / Barriers to Entry
• Unfair competitive advantage
• Intellectual property
• Unique franchise
• Brand, recognition, value, and cost
• First mover advantage, lead time
• Current level of competition
• Future competition
4. Market Risk
• Size of market, now and in the future

• Market growth rate, now and in the future
• Market composition, fragmented or consolidated
• Current market share and projected
• Cyclical market issues
• Market evaluation, historically, currently, exit
5. Technology Risk
• Does it work, when will it work
• Demonstrated features and benefits; real customers
• Sustainable benefits
• Scalability
• Time to completion
• Commercial viability
• Supplier dependency
• Substitution risk
6. Financial Risk
• Availability and cost of capital
• Development before next required round
• Capital required from outside sources
• Burn rate
• Dilution anticipated before liquidity
7. Exit Risk
• Number of potential exits
• Financial buyers
• Strategic buyers
• IPO opportunity
• A creative earnings, DCF
• Cash stream payout
• Future multiples of cash flow

8. ESG Risk
• Environmental
• Social
• Governance

If you're contemplating raising capital for your business, you may want to review this checklist for an internal assessment of the perceived risk that may apply to your business.

ACKNOWLEDGMENTS

This is my first book and writing it was hard, but I am pleased with the fact that I've written it. I would like to thank the folks at Book Launchers for guiding me through the process. I couldn't have done it without your help.

There is nothing that gives me more fulfillment than waking up every day with a clear sense of purpose, but I lost that recently after my wife Terry passed away. We were married for 57 years. She was a special person who stood by and supported me throughout my teaching, coaching and business career, for which I am incredibly grateful.

With the support of my family, writing this book helped me find a renewed purpose. Special thanks go to my daughter Maria Rudnick, my son Brian, and their respective spouses Neal and Jackie for encouraging me to move forward and write this book, and to my grandchildren Macey, Layla, Lyla, and Leighton for giving me the inspiration to do so.

I had the great honor and privilege of working with some truly talented people over the years, many of whom were contributors to this book including: Robert Chefitz, Ed Delia, Jill Diener, Shannon Dolan, Bob Farina, Ben Harrison,

Nigel Hammond, Laura Hills, Rick Kushel, Bob Laurenzo, Michael Santos, Paul Scura, and Jim Weber. Thank you for your wisdom and belief in me.

And finally, I am grateful to those who read this book and pass it on to CEOs and CROs who are building early-stage SaaS companies. Thank you. It will be a valuable resource to them.

ENDNOTES

1 "Software as a Service [SaaS] Market Size & Growth, 2030," Fortune Business Insights, accessed January 25, 2024, https://www.fortunebusiness-sinsights.com/software-as-a-service-saas-market-102222.

2 Neil Patel, "90% Of Startups Fail: Here's What You Need To Know About The 10%," *Forbes*, January 16, 2015, https://www.forbes.com/sites/neilpatel/2015/01/16/90-of-startups-will-fail-heres-what-you-need-to-know-about-the-10/?sh=ea6430666792.

3 "2023 Asia-Pacific Sales Trends Report," HubSpot, accessed January 25, 2024, https://www.hubspot.com/hubfs/HubSpot%20x%20Aircall%20Sales%20Trends%20Report%20+%20APAC%20Spotlight.pdf.

4 "Here's How the Relationship Between B2B Buying, Content, and Sales Reps Has Changed," Worldwide Business Research, accessed January 25, 2024, https://www.wbresearch.com/relationship-between-b2b-buying-content-sales-changed-insights.

5 Mimi An, "Buyers Speak Out: How Sales Needs To Evolve," HubSpot, October 29, 2020, https://blog.hubspot.com/sales/buyers-speak-out-how-sales-needs-to-evolve.

6 Janet Comenos, "How to Structure a Sales Outreach Strategy That Delivers Results," HubSpot, April 13, 2022, https://blog.hubspot.com/sales/b2b-outreach-strategy-for-startups.

7 Nicholas A.C. Read and Stephen J. Bistritz, *Selling to the C-Suite: What Every Executive Wants You to Know About Successfully Selling to the Top* (New York: McGraw-Hill, 2009)

8 Robert B. Miller and Stephen E. Heiman, *Conceptual Selling* (New York: Grand Central Publishing, 1989), page 41

9 Miller and Heiman, Concept Selling, 41

10 Please see appendix A, "Aligning with the Buying Team," and appendix B, "Executive Buyer Conversations" in the Resources and Learning section.

11 TEDx Talks, "Start with Why—How Great Leaders Inspire Action | Simon Sinek | TEDxPugetSound," YouTube, September 28, 2009, video, 18:01, https://www.youtube.com/watch?v=u4ZoJKF_VuA.

12 Simon Sinek, *Start with Why: How Great Leaders Inspire Everyone to Take Action* (New York: Portfolio, 2011).

13 TEDx Talks, "Start with Why."

14 Sinek, *Start with Why*, 37.

15 Miller and Heiman, Conceptual Selling, 45

16 To learn more about how to use the Power Index, see the sections entitled "The Overview and Working Demo" and "Value-based Selling" in the Resource and Learning section.

17 "Here's How the Relationship Between B2B Buying, Content, and Sales Reps Has Changed," Worldwide Business Research, accessed January 25, 2024, https://www.wbresearch.com/relationship-between-b2b-buying-content-sales-changed-insights.

18 See "Value-based Selling" and "Conducting the Working Demo" in the Resources and Learning section.

19 Note: To start, the numbers in red should match the numbers in black (the standard). After each example be sure to change the numbers in red back to the standard.

20 Miller and Heiman, *Conceptual Selling*.